D0525226

FLIGHT EXERCISES

for the Private Pilot's Licence and Associated Ratings

Christopher Leech

The Crowood Press

First published in 2004 by
Airlife Publishing, an imprint of
The Crowood Press Ltd
Ramsbury, Marlborough
Wiltshire SN8 2HR

www.crowood.com

British Library Cataloguing-in-Publication Data
A catalogue record for this book is available from the British Library.

ISBN 1 86126 719 3

Typefaces used: Galliard and Helvetica.

Typeset and designed by
D & N Publishing
Lambourn Woodlands, Hungerford, Berkshire.

Printed and bound in Great Britain by Biddles Ltd, King's Lynn.

CONTENTS

Preface

This book aims to provide a practical and concise guide to the flight exercises for the Aeroplane Private Pilot's Licence and the ratings associated with it, in other words those qualifications that the average recreational or club pilot is likely to be interested in. That being the case, this book should be of interest to the following people:

- Student pilots: Both people taking, or thinking of taking, a course of training for the PPL, and existing licence holders who want to add an additional rating to their licence. Apart from the information on individual exercises, it is hoped to give an overview of the course of training so that the student has an idea of what's involved, where they're going, and how they get there.
- Existing licence and rating holders coming up for renewal and re-test: The Instrument Meteorological Conditions, and Twin ratings, are renewed by formal flight test, while the PPL requires a bi-annual instructional flight. This instructional flight is not a test, but the instructor can refuse to sign off the pilot's log book, if a sufficiently safe standard is not reached. This book provides straightforward and easily accessible revision material for pilots approaching one of these renewals.
- Instructors and flight training organizations: Apart from being a source of instructional material, by including the associated ratings, this book aims to be a marketing tool, encouraging pilots to engage in further training. If that sounds mercenary, it is not meant to be, as more training benefits everybody involved: the student becomes a better pilot, the FTO generates revenue, and for the

wider general aviation community, the more we responsibly exercise our right to 'air navigation' the more likely we are to keep it, squeezed as we are, between the 'NIMBYS' on the one hand and the increasing demands of commercial aviation on the other.

CONVENTIONS USED IN THIS BOOK

In order to help keep the book concise, a number of conventions are used:

⇨ An instruction
☛ A consequence
✈ A theory or airmanship point
☠ Danger or safety
⟳ A decision, as in:
   ⟳ do this
   ⟳ or that

Checklists – Normal Operation

A checklist in a 'sticky label' like this is a normal operation memory checklist, and needs to be learnt by heart.

Emergency Checklist

A checklist in a box like this is an emergency memory checklist, and needs to be learnt by heart.

Introduction

REGULATIONS

The regulatory authority for all civilian aviation in the UK is the Civil Aviation Authority (CAA). The CAA derives its legal authority from a piece of parliamentary legislation called the Air Navigation Order (ANO). While the CAA directly regulates all commercial aviation and most light aircraft flying, responsibility for certain purely 'sporting' forms of aerial activity has been delegated to their own representative bodies, such as the British Microlight Aircraft Association, the British Gliding Association, and so on.

Until relatively recently the CAA issued its own UK licences, which allowed the holder to fly UK ('G' registered) aircraft in the UK and other ICAO states. However, as part of European harmonization, a number of European civil aviation authorities has come together to form the Joint Aviation Authority (JAA), and has agreed to a common set of regulations, the Joint Aviation Requirements (JAR). The CAA now issues JAR licences that allow the holder to operate aircraft registered in any member state. Holders of an existing UK national licence may retain it and have it renewed on expiry; however, all new issues will now be JAR licences, where such a JAR licence exists (but *see* NPPL, below).

The details relating to these licences are set out in a series of documents called *Joint Aviation Requirements – Flight Crew Licensing (JAR-FCL)*. The ones relevant to readers of this book are *JAR-FCL 1* (aeroplanes), and *JAR-FCL 3* (medical requirements). If, for some strange reason, you don't want to plough through these documents yourself, a more digestible version, including the relevant bits of the ANO, is produced yearly by the CAA as a book called *LASORS*, yet another acronym, which stands for *Licensing, Administration and Standardization, Operating Requirements and Safety* (racy title). Training for a JAR-FCL PPL must be carried out in a member state at a Flight Training Organization (FTO) registered for the purpose, although training may be carried out outside the JAA member states at an FTO approved by the civil aviation authority of a member state.

The old CAA PPL course was forty hours long, but with the advent of JAR-FCL this increased to forty-five hours, much to the consternation of some sections of the flight training industry, who felt that this would be a disincentive to potential students. Following considerable lobbying and debate, a new licence, the National Private Pilot's Licence (NPPL) was instituted. The NPPL is administered on behalf of the CAA by a number of sport aviation bodies who collaborated to form the National Pilot's Licensing Group Ltd. At only thirty-two hours, the NPPL is significantly shorter, and therefore cheaper, than the JAR-FCL PPL; however, it only allows flight in UK airspace and has a number of other restrictions. No additional ratings can be added to the NPPL; it can, however, be upgraded to a full JAR-FCL PPL by completing an additional fifteen hours' training. A syllabus is provided for both the JAR PPL and the NPPL in the PPL chapter to allow a comparison to be made.

LICENCES, RATINGS AND DIFFERENCES

Under the JAA scheme of things there are three types of pilot's licence: the Private Pilot's

Licence (PPL), the Commercial Pilot's Licence (CPL), and the Airline Transport Pilot's Licence (ATPL). The type of licence you hold determines the legal and financial scope of your flying; for instance, if you want to earn money as a pilot you need a CPL or an ATPL. In this book, however, we are concerned with the PPL, a recreational pilot's licence that allows the holder to fly as 'pilot in command', but not for remuneration on non-revenue flights, although it may be used as the first step on the road to a higher licence. Ratings, on the other hand, concern the acquisition of a specific skill: this may be the ability to operate a particular class of aeroplane (an aircraft rating), or to be able to fly in different flight conditions such as at night, or in cloud.

So while we commonly talk about doing a PPL course, in actual fact there is no such thing. What you are actually doing is taking an aircraft rating course. Single pilot aeroplanes are divided into 'classes', so you take a course for the particular class of aircraft you want to fly. Since this book is about light aircraft flying, it is assumed the reader will take the 'Single-Engine-Piston (SEP) – land plane' class rating, but there are others, ranging from balloons and airships, to multi-engine or turboprop aircraft (see table opposite). Having completed a class rating course you can then apply for a PPL to be 'opened' on the particular class of aircraft you have learnt to fly. Once the licence has been issued, other classes can be added by taking further courses of training. Generally speaking, to keep a rating current you must either meet an experience (hours) requirement, and/or pass a revalidation flight or test.

Once you have your class rating you are entitled to fly any aircraft within the class. A rating such as the SEP covers a large number of types, from aircraft with simple fixed pitch propellers and fixed undercarriages, to high performance machines that may have turbocharged engines, retractable undercarriages and variable pitch propellers. To cater for this, difference training is required in order to fly a different type within a class, or an aircraft with a greater degree of complexity (see table opposite). Difference training may be very short, maybe only a single flight, and the CAA does not lay down specific syllabi; the instructor simply needs to sign the trainee's log book to show that the training was carried out and that the pilot is now able to cope with whatever the difference is. Difference training on SEP aircraft is valid indefinitely, but on other classes, further training would be required if you haven't flown the variant within two years. Training carried out on a multi-engine piston type covers you for the same variation on an SEP aircraft, but not vice versa.

LEARNING TO FLY

This section aims to provide some guidance for people who are thinking of learning to fly. So do you need lightning fast reactions, vast intelligence, and nerves of steel? Luckily for most pilots the answer is 'no'. Obviously if you possess these abilities you'll get there faster, but even if you don't, provided you have determination and common sense, you'll make it. A good rule of thumb is, if you're clever enough to (legally) raise enough money to pay for your flight training, you're clever enough to learn to fly.

Before you spend too much money, it's worth getting a medical (you will need this before going solo in any event). For professional licences you need a JAR class one medical which, for initial issue, is conducted at the CAA Aeromedical Centre at Gatwick, but for the PPL you only need a class two medical, which can be done by your local friendly CAA Authorized Medical Examiner (AME). Most Flight Training Organizations will have contact details for local AMEs, or alternatively details can be obtained from the CAA-SRG website (www.srg.caa.co.uk). You don't need to be super fit, and there's no problem if you need to wear glasses or contact lenses, provided your eyesight can be corrected to an acceptable standard. For the NPPL the medical standards are based on DVLA criteria, and the certificate can be signed by your own doctor.

You now need to choose a flight training organization (FTO). While I can't make that choice for you, I can point out some of the things you need to be thinking about in order to make that choice for yourself.

Table of Licences, Ratings and Differences	
Licences	
■ *National Private Pilot's Licence*	CAA
■ *Private Pilot's Licence*	JAR-FCL
■ Commercial Pilot's Licence	JAR-FCL
■ Airline Transport Pilot's Licence	JAR-FCL
Aircraft ratings	
■ Balloons	CAA
■ Gyroplanes	CAA
■ Powered parachutes	CAA
■ Microlights	CAA
■ Self-launching motor gliders	CAA
■ Touring motor gliders	JAR-FCL
■ *Single-engine piston (land)*	JAR-FCL
■ Single-engine piston (sea)	JAR-FCL
■ *Multi-engine piston (land)*	JAR-FCL
■ Multi-engine piston (sea)	JAR-FCL
■ Single-engine turbo-prop (land)	JAR-FCL
■ Single-engine turbo-prop (sea)	JAR-FCL
■ Multi-engine turbo-prop (land)	JAR-FCL
■ Multi-engine turbo-prop (sea)	JAR-FCL
■ Multi-engine turbo-jet (land)	JAR-FCL
■ Type ratings for more complex aircraft	JAR-FCL
■ Helicopter ratings	JAR-FCL
Other Ratings	
■ *Night qualification*	JAR-FCL
■ *Instrument meteorological conditions*	CAA
■ Instrument rating	JAR-FCL
■ Instructors rating	JAR-FCL
Differences	
■ Another type in the same class	
■ *Retractable undercarriages*	
■ *Tailwheel*	
■ *Variable pitch propellers*	
■ *Super and turbo charging*	
■ Cabin pressurization	

Items in italics are included in this book.

Flying School or Flying Club

It is perhaps useful to imagine a spectrum. At one end is the FTO that is primarily a flying school, where the emphasis is on training. You could expect a fairly standardized fleet of aircraft, but less interest in hiring out aircraft on a solo basis to individuals who have completed their training. At the other end of the spectrum is the flying club, where the attitude will be more relaxed, and a lot of the flying is done by the members themselves hiring out club aircraft. It may be that any training is something of a sideline. You could expect a rather more diverse fleet of aircraft and a range of other social facilities, such as a club room or bar. Flying and drinking can mix, provided you do them in the right order (anybody having a problem working out what that order should be, should put this book down immediately and consider another hobby). Obviously no two FTOs are the same, and most will fall somewhere between these two extremes.

Big Airport or Little Airfield

All PPL training has to be conducted from a licensed airfield, but these range from large commercial airports to grass strips. If you choose to train at a larger commercial airfield you will be mixing it with commercial airliners, and will become accustomed to a busy and complex 'Air Traffic Control' environment from the start. You will also have to wait around more, since light aircraft tend to take second place to commercial flights – aerodrome operators know which side their bread is buttered. In addition you may have to fly some distance to leave controlled airspace for training to begin, all of which adds to the expense. Flying from a smaller airfield means you don't have to put up with these problems, though when you do go to a bigger airfield the experience is more daunting because you aren't used to it.

Home or Abroad

There are a considerable number of foreign (non-JAA states) FTOs approved to carry out training for JAR-FCL licences, notably in America, but other parts of the world as well. There are two great advantages of this from the student's point of view: the cost, and the weather. As regards cost, lower taxes, particularly on fuel, lower airport charges, and greater utilization rates that spread out the fixed costs, means even when travel and accommodation are taken into account, it will still usually be cheaper to train abroad.

As regards weather, a stable predictable climate guarantees good training conditions.

There is, however, a down side, in that a UK-trained pilot will have gained experience of this country's crowded skies, busy Air Traffic Control environment and, perhaps most importantly, fickle weather while under the watchful eye of his instructors. If you trained abroad you won't have this valuable experience, so don't expect to turn up at your local flying club with a licence you gained in Florida, and be allowed to fly their aircraft without a good few more hours with one of their instructors!

Having weighed up the pros and cons, draw up a shortlist of FTOs. If you're going abroad, personal recommendation is probably your best bet; if training in the UK, go and visit them. Start with local airfields; when you find somewhere you like the look of, book a 'trial lesson'.

You also may wish to consider when to train. Longer daylight hours and better weather means that most training is done in the summer, but don't dismiss winter: a good winter's day can be very good indeed with cold clear skies and superb visibility. The down side is that you are likely to have a lot of flights cancelled due to the weather, which is frustrating; but training in the winter can be very good for those lucky enough to have the flexibility to drop what they're doing at short notice in order to fly when the weather allows. If you get the timing right you could arrange to be ready for licence issue at the beginning of the summer, and get a season's flying experience under your belt in the nice weather before winter sets in again.

CHAPTER 1
Private Pilot's Licence

The Private Pilot's Licence (Single-Engine Piston – Land Plane) course naturally divides into two sections. The first of these involves the 'general handling' of the aeroplane, and further subdivides into 'upper airwork' and 'circuits': 'upper airwork' includes straight and level, climbing and descending, turning, slow flight and stalling. Circuit work is primarily about learning to take off and land, landing being one of the most challenging aspects of learning to fly. When you have achieved proficiency, this part of the course culminates with your first solo and subsequent solo circuit consolidation.

The first solo is an enormously significant milestone in any pilot's training, but it is not, contrary to popular belief, the same as getting a pilot's licence: to do that you have to complete the second part of the course; procedural and navigation training. This involves being able to take an aeroplane, and get safely from A to B, dealing with any problems thrown at you on the way; these might include getting lost; adverse weather; and technical problems such as engine failure. It is in this second part of the course that the syllabuses for the JAR-FCL PPL and the NPPL diverge, as the JAR-FCL course goes into navigation in significantly greater depth, and includes radio navigation, which is not covered at all for the NPPL. Although both licences are for 'visual flight' only, the JAR-FCL course includes 'basic instrument flight', while the NPPL has a more superficial 'instrument appreciation'. It is this greater emphasis on procedure and navigation that equips the JAR-FCL licence holder to operate further afield and abroad. The procedural and navigation part of the course culminates with the 'qualifying cross-country flight', a solo flight of 150nm for the JAR-FCL PPL, or 100nm for the NPPL, with two intermediate landings.

Finally, following some revision, you take the Licence Skill Test; if you are successful, you can then apply for your Private Pilot's Licence.

The above description is inevitably something of a generalization and not exact. There are some discrepancies: Exercise 15, Advanced Turning, is a general handling exercise, but comes after First Solo; however, I think it gives a reasonable overview of the way the training works.

Referring to the syllabus: the exercises are numbered 1 to 19. Some exercises are subdivided, so for example Exercise 18 is Navigation, 18A is Basic Visual Navigation, 18B is Low-Level/Reduced Visibility Navigation, and so on. Some exercises have an emergency section denoted by an 'E', so for example Exercise 5 is Taxiing, Exercise 5E is Taxiing Emergencies.

The exercises follow a logical sequence, and in an ideal world you would complete them in the order given. However, the British weather usually means that some flexibility is required, so for instance on a poor weather day it might not be sensible to do stalling, but it might be possible to do some low-level navigation or instrument flight.

PPL: JAR-FCL Syllabus
Single-Engine Piston Class Rating

FLIGHT TRAINING

Forty-five hours minimum, of which:

- Twenty-five hours dual
- Two hours stall/spin awareness
- Ten hours solo
- Five hours cross country, including one flight of 150nm with two intermediate landings

Flight Exercises

1. Aircraft Familiarization
   1E. Emergency Drills
2. Pre-Flight and After-Flight
3. Air Experience
4. Effects of Controls
5. Taxiing
   5E. Taxiing Emergencies
6. Straight and Level
7. Climbing
8. Descending
9. Turning
10. A. Slow flight ⎫
    B. Stalling   ⎬ Two hours min
11. Spin Avoidance ⎭
12. Take-Off
13. Circuit Approach and Landing
    12/13E. Circuit Emergencies
14. First Solo (medical required)
15. Advanced Turning
16. Forced Landing Without Power
17. Precautionary Landing
18. A. Navigation
    B. Low-Level/Reduced Visibility Nav
    C. Radio Nav
19. Basic Instrument Flight

PPL Skill Test[1]

1. Pre-Flight
2. General Handling
3. Emergency Procedures
4. Circuit
5. Navigation
6. (Type/Class Specific Procedures)

GROUND TRAINING

Ground Examinations (multi-choice, passmark 75%)

- Air Law and Operational Procedures
- Navigation and Radio Aids
- Meteorology
- Aircraft General and Principles of Flight
- Human Performance and Limitations
- Flight Performance and Planning
- Communications/Radio Telephony

Entry to Training

- Age sixteen for solo
- Age seventeen for PPL issue

- ✔ Medical required for solo

Privileges

- ◆ 'Simple' single-engine aeroplanes [2]
- ◆ Day only [2]
- ◆ VMC only [2]
- ◆ Not for 'hire and reward'

[2] Restrictions may be removed by additional training/ratings

---

Validity/Currency

- ✔ Validity: Five years
- ✔ Currency period: Two years
- ✔ Twelve hours in last twelve months of validity period, of which min six hours PIC, including twelve take-offs and landings, and one hour instructional flight [3]
  OR: Proficiency check in last three months of validity
- ✔ Three take-offs and landings in last 90 days for carriage of passengers

[3] May be replaced by any other skill/test

---

[1] Failure in one section only constitutes a Partial Pass, requiring retest of only the failed section. Failure of this retest or failure of more than one section requires complete retest.

NPPL: CAA Syllabus
Single-Engine Piston

FLIGHT TRAINING

Thirty-two hours minimum, of which:

- Twenty-two hours dual
- Air Law and Operational Procedures
- Two hours stall/spin awareness
- One hour instrument appreciation
- Ten hours solo
- Four hours cross country, including one flight of 100nm with two intermediate landings

Flight Exercises

1. Aircraft Familiarization
   1E. Emergency Drills
2. Pre-Flight and After-Flight
3. Air Experience
4. Effects of Controls
5. Taxiing
   5E. Taxiing Emergencies
6. Straight and Level
7. Climbing
8. Descending
9. Medium Turns
10. A. Slow flight
    B. Stalling   } Two hours min
11. Spin Avoidance ⌋
12. Take-Off
13. Circuit Approach Landing
    12/13E. Circuit Emergencies
14. First Solo (medical required)
15. Advanced Turning
16. Forced Landing Without Power
17. Precautionary Landing
18. A. Navigation
    B. Low-Level/Reduced Visibility Nav
19. Instrument Appreciation

Navigational Skill Test [1]

General Skill Test [2]
1. Pre-Flight
2. General Handling
3. Emergency Procedures
4. Circuit

GROUND TRAINING

No specific time limits; may be directed self-study.

Ground Examinations (multi-choice, passmark 75%)

- Navigation and Radio Aids
- Meteorology
- Aircraft General and Principles of Flight
- Human Performance and Limitations
- Flight Performance and Planning
- Communications/Radio Telephony

Entry to Training

- Age sixteen for solo
- Age seventeen for PPL issue

- ✔ Medical required for solo
  (based on DVLA requirements)

Privileges (UK airspace only)

- ◆ 'Simple' single-engine aeroplanes
- ◆ MTOW <2,000kg
- ◆ Day only
- ◆ VMC only
- ◆ Four seats max (i.e. three passengers)
- ◆ Not for 'hire and reward'

Validity/Currency

- ✔ Validity: Lifelong
- ✔ Currency period: Two years
- ✔ Twelve hours in twenty-four months, to include one hour instructional flight, of which six hours in last twelve months of validity period, of which min four hours PIC
  OR: Proficiency check in last three months of validity

---

[1] Must be passed before solo cross country.

[2] Failed sections may be retaken; there is no limit to the number of retests.

PPL FLIGHT EXERCISES (*See* PPL: JAR-FCL Syllabus on page 10)

PPL Exercise 1: Aircraft Familiarization

Exercise 1

Aim: To familiarize the student with a light aircraft.

The Aircraft
- Structure
- Control surfaces
- Ports, probes, vents, intakes and sensors
- Panels and cargo hatches
- Engine compartment

Method of entry

Emergency equipment
- Fire extinguisher
- First-aid kit
- Lifejackets/rafts, flares etc.
- Exits/emergency exits

Internal layout and fittings
- Seats
- Harnesses
- Controls
- Instruments

Method of exit (normal)

Exercise 1E

Aim: To learn the actions to be carried out in the event of fire and other emergencies.

Fire on the Ground

Throttle	Close
⇨ Stop aircraft	
Mixture	Idle cut off
☛ Engine stops	
Fuel/pumps	Off
Mags	Off
(Mayday if time available)	
Master	Off
⇨ Evacuate upwind, taking fire extinguisher with you.	

Engine Fire in Flight

Fuel/pumps	Off
Cabin heaters/air	Closed
☛ Engine stops	
Throttle	Close
Mags	Off
Mixture	Idle cut off
⇨ Forced landing.	

Electrical Fire in Flight

Master	Off
Switches	Off
Heaters and Vents	Close
Fire Extinguisher	Use as necessary
⇨ Ventilate cabin.	

Type-Specific Emergencies
From checklist.

AIRMANSHIP

Security – 'airside' access.
High visibility clothing and aircraft awareness.

PPL Exercise 2: Pre-Flight and After-Flight

Aim: To perform all necessary pre-flight and after-flight actions, and introduce the use of checklists.

Pre-Flight	Checklist Drills	After-Flight
• Weather data • Notams	⇨ Perform as touch drills for familiarization	• Secure aircraft as appropriate to conditions ◆ Chocks ◆ Tie-downs
• Pre-flight briefing • Prepare chart • Complete plog	• External check (walk round) • Internal/before start checks (engine start)	◆ Head into wind ◆ Covers ◆ Lock doors ◆ Hanger
• Fuel calculations • Weight and balance • Performance	• Power checks	• ATC liaison ⇨ Book in/close flight plan
• Tech log ◆ Technical defects ◆ Hours before check ◆ Intended flight details ◆ Authorization	• After landing checks • Shut-down checks	• Tech log ◆ Flight hours and totals ◆ Technical defects
• ATC liaison ⇨ Book out ◆ Registration ◆ Type ◆ Destination/not landing away ◆ Departure route ◆ Flight time ◆ Endurance ◆ Number of POB ⇨ PPR at destination?		• Buy instructor drink at the bar (last flight of the day)
• Prepare aircraft ⇨ Remove chocks and covers ⇨ Check or complete fuelling ⇨ Load aircraft ⇨ Passenger safety brief		

AIRMANSHIP

Call 'Clear prop' before engine start.
Position aircraft to avoid prop-wash damage and allow easy taxi out.

PPL Exercise 3: Air Experience

Aim: To experience flight in a light aircraft.

Controls	Movement	Primary Effect	Secondary Effect
Elevator	Control column: forward/back	Nose up or down (pitch)	Airspeed/Height
Ailerons	Control column: side to side	Roll	Turns aeroplane
Rudder	Pedals: left/right	Nose side to side (yaw)	Turns aeroplane
All effects are in relation to the pilot/axis of the aircraft, not the horizon.			

Attitude

Look at the horizon   ⇨ Position nose relative to the horizon.

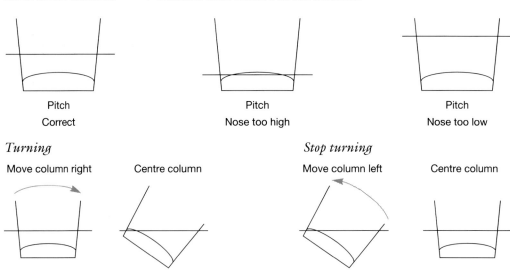

| Pitch | Pitch | Pitch |
| Correct | Nose too high | Nose too low |

Turning   *Stop turning*

Move column right   Centre column   Move column left   Centre column

✈ To fly in a straight line, the wings must be level.

AIRMANSHIP

Lookout
Following through
Hand over: 'You have control.'   'I have control.'

PPL Exercise 4: Effects of Controls 1

Aim: To learn the effects of the aircraft's primary controls.

The aircraft's primary controls consist of the control column or yoke and the rudder pedals, which between them control the aircraft's movement in three planes:

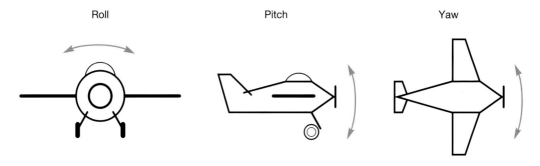

Controls	Movement	Primary Effect	Secondary Effect
Elevator	Control column: forward/back	Pitch	Airspeed/Height (*see* note below)
Ailerons	Control column: side to side/turn	Roll	Yaw
Rudder	Pedals: left/right	Yaw	Roll
All effects are in relation to the pilot/axis of the aircraft, not the horizon.			

The secondary effects of pitch are as follows:

- Pitch nose up ☛ Airspeed reduces – height increases.
- Pitch nose down ☛ Airspeed increases – height reduces.

Response Rate

⇨ Initiate a roll using the control column:

- Small control input   ☞ The aircraft responds slowly.
- Large control input   ☞ The aircraft responds quickly.

- Slow control input   ☞ Little effect on response rate.
- Quick control input   ☞ Little effect on response rate.

➤ The response rate of the aircraft depends on the amount of control input, not how fast you do it. (The same applies to rudder and elevator inputs.)

Effect of Airspeed and Power on Controls

Power (Constant Airspeed)	Low	High
Configuration	Idle power descent (70kts)	Full power climb (70kts)
Response	Elevator and rudder sloppy, ailerons not affected	Elevator and rudder firm, ailerons not affected

➤ The elevator and rudder responses are affected by the power setting; however, the ailerons are not affected as they do not lie within the propeller slipstream.

Airspeed (Constant Power)	Low	High
Configuration	Power: 1,900rpm ⇨ Attitude to achieve 65kts	Power: 1,900rpm ⇨ Attitude to achieve 100kts
Response	All controls firm	All controls sloppy

➤ All the control surfaces are affected by the amount of airflow over them due to airspeed.

AIRMANSHIP	ENGINE HANDLING
Lookout Checklist Hand over Booking out	Smooth operation of throttle

PPL Exercise 4: Effects of Controls 2

Aim: To learn the effects of the auxiliary controls.

Engine Control

Throttle
Controls power:
- Power setting indicated on RPM gauge.
→ Green arc indicates power setting where carb heat is required.

    ⇨ Increase power   ☛ pitch up   ☛ yaw/roll left.
    ⇨ Decrease power   ☛ pitch down   ☛ yaw/roll right.
- Airspeed stays approximately constant.

    Note: Increase airspeed   ☛ increase RPM.
                   Decrease airspeed   ☛ decrease RPM.

Carburettor heat
Directs hot air through the carburettor to prevent/remove ice build-up:
→ Treat as on/off switch.
    ⇨ Leave on for five to ten seconds.
    ☛ Expect a small drop in RPM.

    ☠ If a large RPM drop is experienced you have icing.
        ⇨ Leave the carb heat ON until RPM recovers.

Mixture
Controls fuel/air mixture.
    ⇨ Slowly retard the mixture control.
        ☛ Initially RPM rises, then falls.
    ⇨ As soon as a fall is noticed, move the mixture control slightly forward to achieve peak RPM.

    → Lean mixture with increasing altitude.

Flight Controls

Trim

    Neutralizes unwanted forces on the controls:
- ⇨ Adjust pitch attitude with the control column.
- ⇨ Trim to reduce load on the control column.
  - ⇨ Wind trim in the same direction as the control column force.
- ✈ Pitch attitude should not change as the aircraft is trimmed.

Flaps

    Increase the wings' lift and drag:
- ✈ Airspeed should be below V_{fe} – white arc
- ⇨ Lower flaps in stages   ☛ pitch up
  or if constant attitude maintained
  ☛ decreasing airspeed.
- ⇨ Raise flaps in stages   ☛ pitch down
  or if constant attitude maintained
  ☛ increasing airspeed.
- ✈ Initially the aircraft may sink until airspeed is regained.

Setting	Lift	Drag
10°	Increased	Increased
20°	Increased	Increased
30°	Slightly increased	Greatly increased
Flap settings > 20° usually referred to as 'drag flap'.		

AIRMANSHIP	ENGINE HANDLING
Lookout – clock code V_{fe} – white arc Checks/checklist	Smooth Carb heat

PPL Exercise 5: Taxiing

Aim: To manoeuvre the aircraft safely on the ground.

Taxiing Technique

Speed control
⇨ Higher power to move off.
⇨ Control speed with throttle, then brake.
✈ Avoid use of power against brake.

Turning
⇨ Use rudder pedals.
⇨ Use differential brake if necessary in confined spaces.
   ✈ Generally avoid the use of differential brake where possible.

Stopping
⇨ Close throttle first, then brake.
⇨ Stop with nose-wheel straight.
⇨ Nose into wind (if strong and for power check).
⇨ Once stopped, set idle at approximately 1,200rpm.

General points
• Grass to concrete transition at 45°, different amounts of power needed.
• Taxi on rough surface with control yoke back to unload nose-wheel.
• In strong winds put into wind, control surface down.
• Remember wingspan and effect of pivot point on tail movement.

Taxi Checks

Brake		(in clear area)
Turn:		nose-wheel steering
	Left	Compass/DI – decreasing
	Right	Compass/DI – increasing
	AI	level
	TC	turn indicated

PPL Exercise 5E: Taxiing Emergencies

Aim: To deal with emergencies on the ground.

Taxiing Techniques

Nose-wheel steering failure
⇨ Control direction with use of differential brake.
⇨ Taxi to safe parking area.
⇨ Shut down.

Brake failure
⇨ Close throttle.
⇨ Steer for open area/grass.
⇨ Shut down.
⇨ Inform ATC.

Fire on Ground

Throttle	Close
⇨ Stop aircraft	
Mixture	Idle cut off
☛ Engine stops	
Fuel/pumps	Off
Mags	Off
('Mayday' if time available)	
Master	Off
⇨ Evacuate upwind, taking fire extinguisher with you.	

AIRMANSHIP	ENGINE HANDLING
Flaps up	Carb heat off
Prop wash	Idle at 1,200rpm

PPL Exercise 6: Straight and Level 1

Aim: To fly the aircraft at a constant height and heading (in balance).

POWER   Standard cruise power setting

ATTITUDE

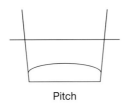

Pitch

Position nose relative to horizon.
⇨ Use elevators.

Wings level:
⇨ Use aileron.

Balance ball central:
⇨ Use rudder.

TRIM To remove control load.

FREDA

Fuel	Tank/pump/sufficient
Radio	Freq/standby
Engine	Ts and Ps
	Carb heat
Direction indicator	Synchronized
Altimeter	Pressure setting

Power + Attitude = Performance

Performance
1. Visual reference:
   Level – relative to the horizon.
   Straight – relative to a prominent object
   on the horizon.
2. Instrument scan:
   Level – altimeter/vertical speed indicator.
   Straight – direction indicator/compass.
   Speed – airspeed indicator.
   RPM – Will fluctuate slightly as attitude changes:
   ⇨ reset as necessary.

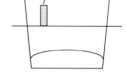

Scan
✦ Two-thirds outside; one-third instruments.

Corrections
✦ Don't chase the instruments!
   ⇨ Make small corrections relative to the visual horizon.
   ⇨ Wait.
   ⇨ Scan instruments to confirm the effect of the correction.
   ⇨ Make further corrections as necessary:
   • Altitude ± 100ft.
   • Hdg ± 10°.
   • Speed ± 10kts.

AIRMANSHIP	ENGINE HANDLING
Lookout **FREDA**	Readjust RPM as necessary

PPL Exercise 6: Straight and Level 2

Aim: To fly the aircraft at a constant height and heading (in balance) at different airspeeds and different configurations.

	POWER	**ATTITUDE**	**TRIM**
FAST			

High RPM

To remove control load.

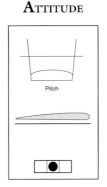

☛ **Performance** – high speed, level flight.

SLOW

Low RPM

To remove control load.

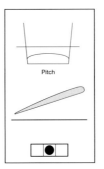

☛ **Performance** – low speed, level flight.

⇨ Reduce speed further
   ☛ 'Back of drag curve'.

High RPM
   ☛ To counter
      increased drag at
      high angle of attack.

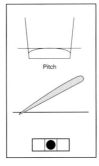

☛ **Performance** – very low speed, level flight.

Effects of Lowering and Raising Flaps

Entry	During	Recovery
1. Flap lowering: Clean straight and level flight ⇨ reduce speed to V_{fe} – white arc – if necessary ⇨ Lower flap one stage at a time	Note: ■ Pitch up ■ Airspeed reduction	⇨ Adjust attitude to maintain level flight ⇨ Trim Note: ■ Lower nose attitude ■ Higher power required for a given airspeed
2. Flap raising: Straight and level flight with full flap ⇨ Raise flaps in stages	Note: ■ Pitch down ■ Airspeed increases ■ Aircraft may sink until airspeed is regained	⇨ Adjust attitude to maintain level flight ⇨ Trim ⇨ Recover to clean straight and level flight Note: ■ If original power setting is retained, original speed should be regained

Use of flap allows:

➜ the aircraft to fly more slowly/at a better margin above stall speed;
➜ better forward visibility during slow flight due to lower nose attitude.

AIRMANSHIP	ENGINE HANDLING
Lookout – high-nose attitude **FREDA** V_{fe} – white arc	Readjust RPM as necessary

PPL Exercise 7: Climbing 1

Aim: To gain height at a constant airspeed (in balance).

Entry	During	Recovery

Power
   Full   [⬤]
 	
 Attitude
 	
 (Pitch diagram)
 	
 Pitch
 	
 ⇨ To achieve:
   Best rate of climb
   airspeed: V_y
 	
 Trim
	Lookout
	 ✈ Weave nose of aircraft 10°
	   either side of desired
	   heading to allow
	   forward vision
	
	 Check:
	 ▪ Gauges – engine
	 ▪ Direction indicator
	 ▪ Airspeed indicator
	
	 Note:
	 ▪ Rate of climb
		Attitude
		   Straight and level
		   ⇨ Wait
		   ☛ Cruise airspeed
		
		 Power [⬤]
		   Cruise power setting
		
		 Trim

Lookout during the climb

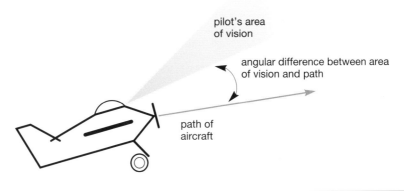

pilot's area of vision

angular difference between area of vision and path

path of aircraft

AIRMANSHIP	ENGINE HANDLING
Lookout – difficult in climb	Monitor Ts and Ps

PPL Exercise 7: Climbing 2

Aim: To learn the effect of flap and speed changes on climb performance.

1. Flap

Entry	During	Recovery
As Climbing 1	As Climbing 1	1. To clean climb

Note:
■ Rate of climb
	Note:
	■ Reduce rate of climb
	■ Lower nose attitude
	  (especially full flap)
		Raise flaps in stages
		
		Attitude
		⇨ Maintain airspeed
		⇨ Then return to V_y as last
		  stage of flap is raised

Lower flaps in stages		
Attitude ⇨ Maintain airspeed ⇨ The reduce to V_y−5kts		2. To straight and level – as Climbing 1

2. Deviation from V_y

Entry	During	Recovery
Best rate of climb: as Climbing 1		1. To normal climb

Attitude
⇨ To achieve:
  V_y +5kts, +10kts
  V_y −5kts, −10kts
	Note:
	■ Reduction in rate
	  of climb
		Attitude
		⇨ To achieve V_y
		
		Note:
		■ Increased rate of climb
		
		2. To straight and level –
		  as Climbing 1

AIRMANSHIP	ENGINE HANDLING
Lookout – difficult in climb	Monitor Ts and Ps

PPL Exercise 8: Descending 1

Aim: To descend at a specified airspeed (in balance).

Entry	During	Recovery
Cruise descent Carb heat – on **P**ower 　1,900rpm **A**ttitude Pitch ⇨ To maintain: 　Cruise airspeed **T**rim	**Lookout** Check ▪ Direction indicator ▪ Airspeed indicator ☠ Warm engine 　⇨ Every 500ft Note: ▪ Rate of descent	Anticipate level-out altitude by 50ft Carb heat – off **P**ower 　Cruise power setting **A**ttitude 　Straight and level **T**rim
Glide descent Carb heat – on **P**ower 　Idle **A**ttitude ⇨ To achieve: 　Best glide airspeed **T**rim	As above ☠ Warm engine 　⇨ Every 500ft Note: ▪ Rate of descent	As above

AIRMANSHIP	ENGINE HANDLING
Lookout	Warm engine/carb heat

PPL Exercise 8: Descending 2

Aim: To learn the effect of power, speed, flaps and sideslip on descent.

1. Power

Entry	During	Recovery

As Descending 1
 	
Enter cruise descent:
  Power
    1,900rpm
  Attitude
   ⇨ Maintain airspeed
  Trim
	As Descending 1
	
	Note:
	■ Rate of descent
	
	⇨ Reduce power
	    (1,900rpm to idle)
	⇨ Maintain airspeed
	
	Note:
	■ Increased rate of descent
		As Descending 1

✈ For a given constant airspeed, power controls the rate of descent:
- power increased   ☛ rate of descent decreased;
- power decreased   ☛ rate of descent increased.

2. Speed

Entry	During	Recovery

As Descending 1
 	
Enter glide descent:
  Power
    Idle
  Attitude
   ⇨ Best glide airspeed
  Trim
	As Descending 1
	
	Note:
	■ Rate of descent
	
	⇨ Increase airspeed
	⇨ Maintain power setting
	
	Note:
	■ Increased rate of descent
		As Descending 1

✈ For a given constant power setting, airspeed controls the rate of descent:

- airspeed increased   ☛ rate of descent increased;
- airspeed decreased   ☛ rate of descent decreased.

3. Flap

Entry	During	Recovery
As Descending 1 Note: ■ Rate of descent Lower flaps in stages Adjust attitude ⇨ Maintain airspeed	As Descending 1 Note: ■ Increased rate of descent ■ Lower nose attitude	1. To clean descent Raise flap in stages Adjust attitude ⇨ Maintain airspeed 2. To straight and level – as Descending 1

4. Sideslip

Entry	During	Recovery
As Descending 1 Note: ■ Rate of descent Apply bank ⇨ Aileron Prevent yaw ⇨ Opposite rudder	As Descending 1 Note: ■ ++ Increased rate of descent ■ ++ Lower nose attitude	1. To clean descent ⇨ Centralize rudder ⇨ Wings level 2. To straight and level – as Descending 1

✈ Flap and sideslip both increase the rate of descent.

AIRMANSHIP	ENGINE HANDLING
Lookout	Warm engine/carb heat

SUMMARY OF CLIMB AND DESCENT PROCEDURES

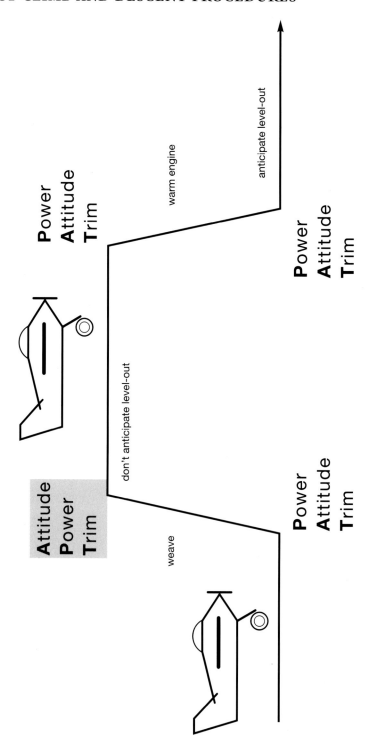

PPL Exercise 9: Turning 1

Aim: To change heading at a constant rate and height (in balance).

Entry	During	Recovery
Bank – 30°	Lookout	**B**ank – level
Balance	Maintain BBB	**B**alance
Back pressure ⇨ Maintain height	➜ Use nose attitude against horizon to maintain height Note: ▪ Speed loss < 5kts	**B**ack pressure – release ⇨ Cruise airspeed

Lookout

➜ Before starting a turn, complete a full inspection of the visible sky, starting in
the direction away from the turn, and finishing in the direction of the turn.
➜ In high-wing aircraft, initially raise the wing in the direction of the turn to increase
visibility.

Speed Loss in the Turn

➜ The vertical component of lift is reduced when the aircraft banks.
☛ Pitch attitude is increased to regain lost lift (back pressure).
☛ Increased drag causes a small loss of airspeed.

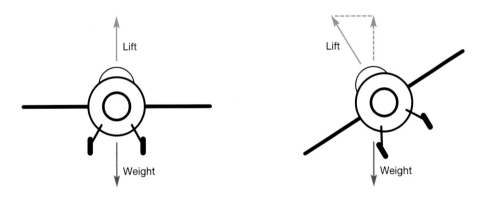

AIRMANSHIP

Lookout – Lift wing (high-wing aircraft)

PPL Exercise 9: Turning 2

Aim: To execute climbing and descending turns.

1. Climbing Turn

Entry	During	Recovery
From straight climb **B**ank – 15° **B**alance *No* back pressure ⇨ Maintain airspeed	Maintain: • Airspeed • Balance Note: ▪ Reduced rate of climb	As Turning 1 1. To straight climb 2. To straight and level

✈ Turning decreases the rate of climb.

2. Descending Turn

Entry	During	Recovery
From straight descent **B**ank – 30° **B**alance *No* back pressure ⇨ Maintain airspeed	Maintain: • Airspeed • Balance Note: ▪ Increased rate of descent	As Turning 1 1. To straight descent 2. To straight and level

✈ Turning increases the rate of descent.

AIRMANSHIP

Lookout
Maintenance of airspeed

PPL Exercise 10A: Slow Flight

Aim: To learn to recognize, control and recover from inadvertent flight at critically low air-speed, and thus avoid a stall or a spin.

Entry	During	Recovery
Power Low power to decelerate **A**ttitude ⇨ To maintain straight and level at V_{si} + 10kts ✈ Increase power to maintain level flight **T**rim	Maintain straight and level Reduce speed by 5kt Note: ▪ Sloppy controls ▪ High nose attitude ▪ Low airspeed ▪ Stall warner ▪ Low noise ▪ Buffet Enter turn Note: ▪ More power needed to maintain airspeed ▪ Large rudder input to maintain balance	**P**ower Full until normal cruise speed Then cruise power **A**ttitude Straight and level ⇨ Maintain balance as speed builds. **T**rim

Effect of Flap

Repeat the exercise.
⇨ Lower flaps in stages.
⇨ Adjust power to achieve V_{so} + 5kts

Note:
• Needs more power
  ☛ Controls more effective and higher noise level.
• Lower nose attitude
  ☛ Better forward visibility.

AIRMANSHIP	ENGINE HANDLING
Lookout	Carb heat

PPL Exercise 10B: Stalling 1

Aim: To learn to recognize, and recover from, a stall.

Entry	During	Recovery

HASELL (*see* box below)
Note:
■ Start altitude
 	
Power
    Idle
 	
Maintain altitude
⇨ Raise nose
✈ Use VSI
 	
Balance
	Note:
	■ G brake
	■ High rate of descent
	■ Low airspeed
	■ Buffet
		⇨ **S**tick forward
		⇨ **F**ull power
		⇨ **O**pposite rudder
		    ✈ Enough to arrest
		        wing drop only
		
		✈ Recover to climb

Wing Drop at the Stall

- Due to lack of balance:
⇨ Use the opposite rudder to arrest wing drop – *not to level the wing!*
✈ Ailerons used to level the wing *only* when a safe flying speed is achieved.

HASELL

Height	Sufficient to recover by 2,500ft
Airframe	As required
Security	Hatches/harnesses/ loose articles
Engine	Ts and Ps/carb heat
Location	Clear of cloud/controlled airspace/built-up areas
Lookout	Especially below – clearing turns.

Symptoms of a Stall

1. Low airspeed
2. Stall warner
3. High nose attitude
4. Poor control
5. Buffet
6. Low noise

AIRMANSHIP	**ENGINE HANDLING**
HASELL Orientation	Carb heat Smooth application of power

PPL Exercise 10B: Stalling 2

Aim: To learn to recognize, and recover from, the stall in the approach configuration, and during a turn.

Entry	During	Recovery

1. Approach configuration
 	
HASELL/HELL
 	
Power
   1,700rpm
 	
⇨ Flap 20°
 	
Attitude
⇨ Raise nose to maintain
   altitude
 	
Balance `[  ●  ]`
	Note:
	■ Sharper G brake
	■ + Wing drop tendency
		Recovery at Incipient Stage
		
		⇨ Stick forward
		   ✈ To achieve level
		     flight only
		   ☛ Minimum height loss
		⇨ Full power
		⇨ Opposite rudder
		   ✈ Arrest wing drop
		     only
		
		⇨ Recover to climb

2. Turn
 	
HASELL/HELL
 	
Enter medium level turn
 	
Power
   1,700rpm
 	
Attitude
⇨ Raise nose to maintain
   altitude
 	
Balance `[  ●  ]`
	Note:
	■ + Wing drop tendency
		⇨ Stick forward
		⇨ Full power
		⇨ Opposite rudder
		   ✈ Arrest wing drop
		     only
		
		⇨ Level wing with aileron
		   only once safe airspeed
		   achieved
		⇨ Recover to climb

✈ HELL (an abbreviated HASELL) check can be used before subsequent stalling attempts, having done the full HASELL check initially.

AIRMANSHIP	ENGINE HANDLING
HASELL/HELL Orientation	Carb heat Smooth application of power

PPL Exercise 11: Spin Avoidance

Aim: To learn to recognize the approach to, and recover from, a spin at the incipient stage.

Entry	During	Recovery
HASELL Power 1,700rpm Entry as clean stall Wing drop at G brake (induced by instructor as necessary)	Note: ■ ++ Wing drop ■ Yaw into spin ✈ Turn co-ordinator always shows direction	⇨ Close throttle ⇨ Stick forward ⇨ Opposite rudder ☛ Aircraft will enter dive ⇨ Level wing with aileron once safe airspeed achieved At V_y ⇨ *Gently* pull back on control yoke ⇨ Smoothly apply power ⇨ Recover to climb

AIRMANSHIP	**ENGINE HANDLING**
HASELL Extra height required at entry Orientation Clean airframe	Carb heat Smooth application of power

CIRCUITS

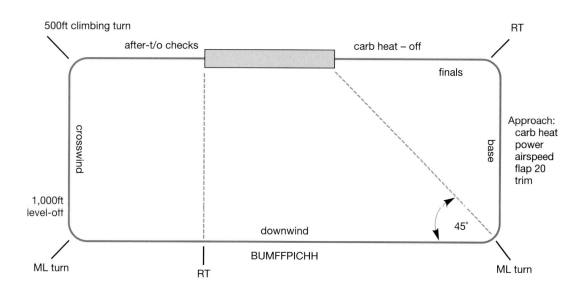

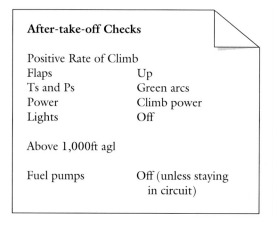

After-take-off Checks

Positive Rate of Climb
Flaps	Up
Ts and Ps	Green arcs
Power	Climb power
Lights	Off

Above 1,000ft agl

Fuel pumps	Off (unless staying in circuit)

BUMFFPICHH

Brakes	Off
Undercarriage	Down
Mixture	Rich
Fuel	Sufficient/pumps on
Flaps	As required
Pitch	Fixed/max RPM
Instruments	Set QFE
Carb heat	Checked hot
Hatches	Secure
Harnesses	Secure

PPL Exercise 12: Take-off and Climb to Downwind

Aim: To learn to take off, and to perform the initial climb out.

Take-off

Runway holding point

Power and pre-take-off checks
Call 'Ready for departure'

Cleared to line up

Lookout along approach
Line up
Check that heading matches runway
   designation

Cleared for take-off

Into-wind aileron
Full power
⇨ Balance
Check
   • RPM
   • Ts and Ps
   • airspeed
Back pressure: weight off nosewheel

V_r

Rotate
Climb at V_y
After-take-off checks

Climb to Downwind

500ft agl

Climbing turn on to crosswind leg

1,000ft agl

Level out
Medium level turn on to downwind leg

AIRMANSHIP	ENGINE HANDLING
Lookout/Listen out – Situational awareness Crosswind effects and limits	Engine warm (Ts and Ps in green arc) before high power is applied

PPL Exercise 13: Circuit, Approach and Landing

Aim: To fly a circuit and be able to land a light aircraft.

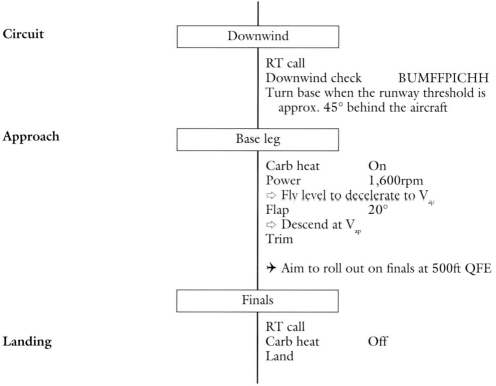

Circuit

Downwind

RT call
Downwind check   BUMFFPICHH
Turn base when the runway threshold is
    approx. 45° behind the aircraft

Approach

Base leg

Carb heat   On
Power   1,600rpm
⇨ Fly level to decelerate to V_{ap}
Flap   20°
⇨ Descend at V_{ap}
Trim

→ Aim to roll out on finals at 500ft QFE

Finals

RT call
Landing   Carb heat   Off
Land

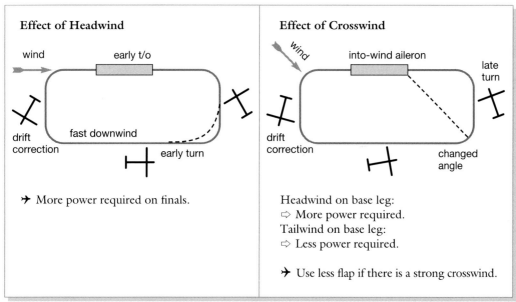

Effect of Headwind

wind   early t/o

drift
correction   fast downwind   early turn

→ More power required on finals.

Effect of Crosswind

wind   into-wind aileron   late
                                         turn

drift
correction   changed
                              angle

Headwind on base leg:
⇨ More power required.
Tailwind on base leg:
⇨ Less power required.

→ Use less flap if there is a strong crosswind.

Approach

- **Pitch controls speed**
  ⇨ **Constant speed: V$_{ap}$**

- **Power controls height**

Scan
- Runway threshold
- Airspeed indicator

ok

high

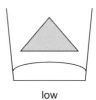

low

Crosswind Approach Techniques

1. Crabbing	2. Wing Down (Sideslip)
At touchdown	At touchdown
⇨ Align to runway with rudder ⇨ Use ailerons to maintain wings level	⇨ Wings level Note • + Rate of Descent

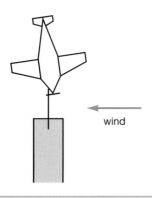

wind

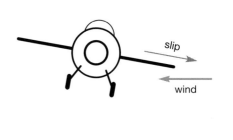

slip

wind

Landing

flare

| Arrest descent approx. 20ft | Slow straight and level | Close throttle – sink Hold off – nose up | Main wheels touch |

Orbits
⇨ 15° bank.
⇨ Away from runway.
✈ Beware of drift.

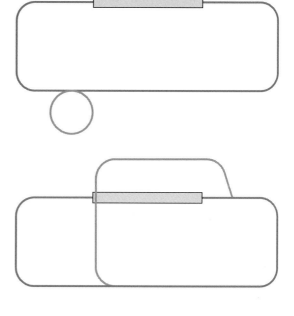

Go around
• Power   Full
• Attitude
  ⇨ To achieve best climb speed:
     V_y
(raise drag flap).
• Trim.

⇨ RT call.
⇨ Break to dead side.
⇨ Raise flaps in stages above 300ft.
⇨ Climb to circuit height, cross
    runway end to rejoin downwind.

Short/soft field take-off
• Flap (type specific):
⇨ Back pressure to lift off at
   minimum airspeed.
⇨ Accelerate level to climb airspeed
    ⇨ V_x until obstacles cleared,
    ⇨ then V_y

Flapless approach
⇨ Approach speed 5kts higher
   than normal.
Note:
▪ Flat/nose-high approach;
▪ Poor visibility on approach.

Short/soft field landing
⇨ Full flap on finals.
⇨ Reduce landing speed by 5kts.

Glide approach
⇨ Base turn abeam threshold:
✈ Only use flaps when sure
   of reaching threshold;
✈ Take account of wind.

AIRMANSHIP	**ENGINE HANDLING**
Local noise restrictions **BUMFFPICHH**	Carb heat

PPL Exercises 12 & 13E: Circuit Emergencies

Aim: to deal with problems in the circuit.

Coping with Problems

Engine Failure After Take-Off (EFATO)

- Attitude
  ⇨ To achieve the best glide airspeed.
- Trim

⇨ Select field within 30° of nose.
☠ *Do not turn back!*

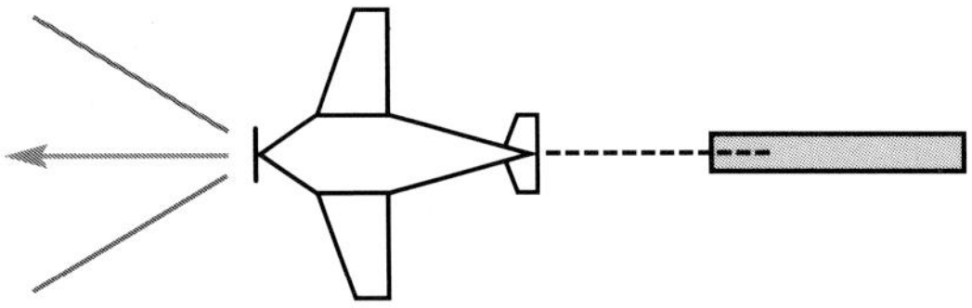

✈ Mayday
Checks: (touch drills)

- (carb heat)
- Mixture ICO
- Fuel Off
- Mags Off
- Master Off
  (if electric flaps – leave on until final flap selection)

⇨ Flaps As required
⇨ Door ajar

Balloon/Bounce

⇨ Full power.
⇨ Go around.

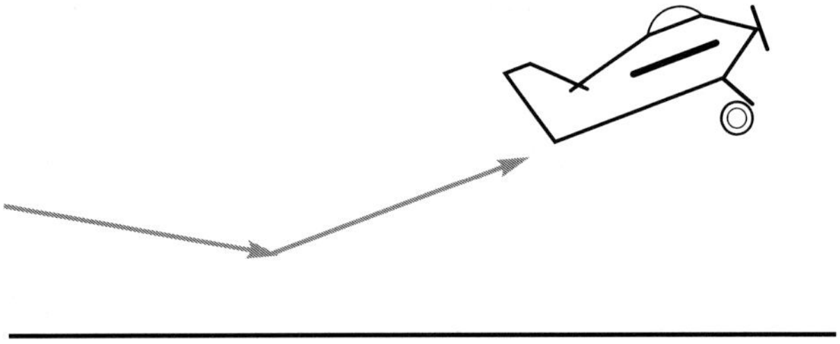

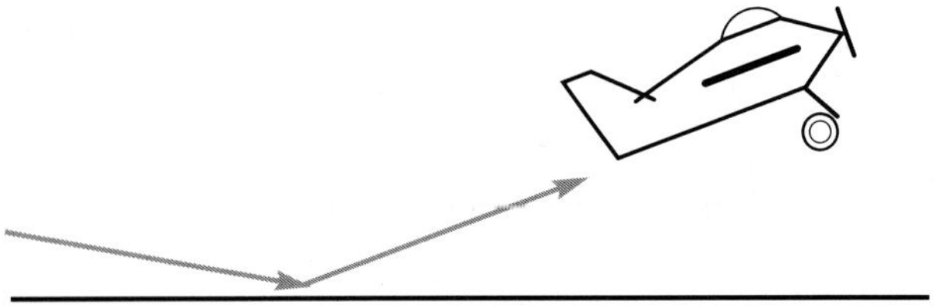

AIRMANSHIP	ENGINE HANDLING
Knowledge of suitable landing areas for EFATO	Checks Ts and Ps at take-off

PPL Exercise 14: First Solo

Ideal conditions for a first solo flight would be a clear day with a cloud base well above circuit height, and a light wind (10kts or less) within 30° of the runway heading. The usual procedure is to do a number of circuits with the instructor, who, when he's satisfied, will ask you to taxi to a safe place for him to disembark. He will then inform Air Traffic Control that it's your first solo, and instruct you to do one single circuit.

Once the instructor is safely away from the aircraft, reset idle power and get taxi instructions. Perform the power and pre-flight checks at the holding point, and you're ready to go! Because the aircraft is lighter without the instructor, it will climb more quickly so you will reach circuit height earlier in the pattern; it may also float a bit more on landing. The important thing is to *fly the airspeeds you have been taught* and you'll be fine.

It's normal to be a bit apprehensive before a first solo, but everybody who has been there will tell you that once cleared for take-off, the next ten minutes feel like about thirty seconds, and you're much too busy to feel worried.

Congratulations! You are now entitled to feel a considerable sense of achievement.

Solo Consolidation

You now need to build up to three or four hours of solo circuit time. At first you can expect to have to do a few circuits with an instructor before being allowed to do a similar number by yourself, but eventually you will just be given an aircraft and told to go and 'bash' the circuit for an hour or so.

AIRMANSHIP

Fly the aeroplane:

Airspeed!   Airspeed!   Airspeed!

PPL Exercise 15: Advanced Turning

Aim: To turn the aircraft at high angles of bank.

1. Steep Level Turn

Entry	During	Recovery

Bank – 45°
 	
Balance
 	
Back pressure + +
⇨ Maintain height
 	
As bank > 30°
⇨ **I**ncrease power
	Lookout
	
	Maintain BBB
	
	✈ Use nose attitude against
	  horizon to maintain
	  height.
	
	Adjust power as required
	⇨ Maintain airspeed
		Bank – level
		
		Balance
		
		Back pressure – release
		
		As bank < 30°
		⇨ **D**ecrease power to
		  cruise

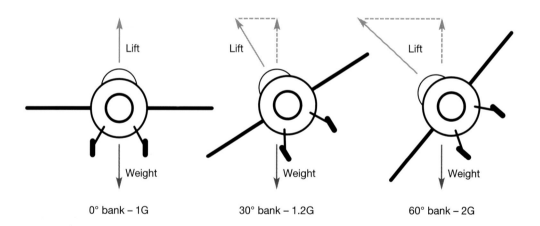

0° bank – 1G   30° bank – 1.2G   60° bank – 2G

☠ The aircraft is nearer the stall at high 'g' at high angles of bank:
  ☛ Speed must not be allowed to decay;
    ⇨ Use increased power to maintain airspeed.

2. Steep Descending Turn

Entry	During	Recovery
From straight glide descent **B**ank – 45° **B**alance As bank > 30° ⇨ Lower nose 　⇨ Maintain airspeed	Lookout Maintain bank and balance ✈ Use nose attitude to 　maintain airspeed Note: ■ + Increased rate of 　descent	**B**ank – level **B**alance As bank < 30° ⇨ Raise nose 　⇨ Maintain airspeed Recover to level flight

Spiral Dive

Symptoms
  Nose down attitude
  High rate of descent
  Rotation
  High airspeed

Recovery
  Level wings – ailerons
  Pull out of dive

Spin

Symptoms
  Nose down attitude
  High rate of descent
  Rotation
  Low airspeed (stall warner)

Recovery
  Close throttle
  Stick forward
  Full opposite rudder
  Pull out of dive

AIRMANSHIP

Lookout – lift wing
Start high in descending turn due to
the large height loss expected

PPL Exercise 16: Forced Landing Without Power

Aim: To land safely in the event of an engine failure.

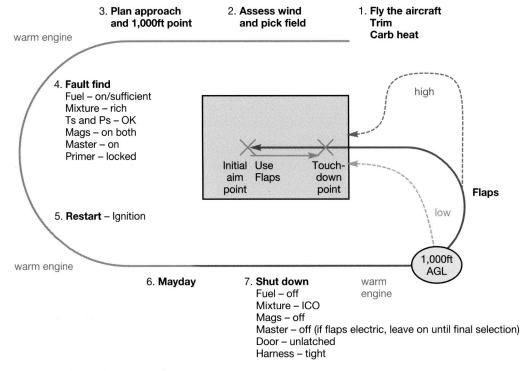

Pattern and Height

- Height >1,500ft   As above

- Height 1,500ft to 500ft
  ⇨ Turn 90° to wind to orientate (base leg).
  ⇨ Look for field ahead and left/right
     (depending on wind direction).
  ⇨ Complete above pattern from the
     1,000ft point.

- Height < 500ft   EFATO

Field Selection

Shape
Size
Surface
Slope
Surround
(Surface wind)

AIRMANSHIP	ENGINE HANDLING
Fly the aeroplane (Aviate – navigate – communicate) Low flying rules	Warm engine Carb heat

PPL Exercise 17: Precautionary Landing (Forced Landing with Power)

Aim: To be able to carry out an unscheduled landing away from an airfield.

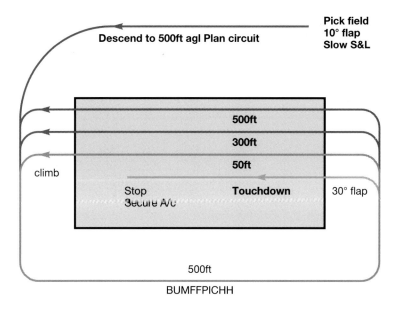

First Pass	500ft agl	Undershoot/overshoot Field conditions Pylons
Second Pass	300ft agl	Domestic cables Slope Minor obstructions
Third Pass	50ft agl	Surface detail Electric fences
Fourth Pass		Land

☠ **The need for this is mostly self induced!**
→ Don't go in the first place!
→ Turn back!
→ Divert!

AIRMANSHIP

Lookout
Inform ATC
Low flying rules

PPL Exercise 18A: Navigation

Aim: To navigate cross-country and join an aerodrome traffic pattern safely.

Planning/Pre-flight	En route	Arrival/Post flight

Weather
Notams
 	
Prepare chart
■ Route/waypoints
■ Terrain
■ Controlled airspace etc.
 	
Complete Plog
■ Hdg and time calculations
■ Altitude/safety altitude
■ Radio/nav. frequencies
■ Fuel calculations
 	
Weight and balance
Performance
 	
Tech Log
 	
ATC liaison
■ Book out
■ PPR
 	
Prepare aircraft
	Aviate
	⇨ Fly aeroplane
	⇨ Perform checks
	   ✈ (Carb heat)
	
	Navigate
	⇨ Map reading
	⇨ Maintain course
	   ✈ (Re-set DI regularly)
	⇨ Complete Plog
	⇨ Fuel burn
	
	Communicate
	⇨ RT
		Approach checks
		
		ATC
		⇨ Joining instructions
		   ☠ (before entering
		      controlled airspace)
		⇨ Weather info.
		
		Joining
		⇨ As directed by ATC
		Or:
		⇨ Overhead join
		
		2,000ft QFE ——————
		Descending - - - - - - -
		Circuit height ————
		
		Post flight
		■ Secure aircraft
		■ Book in
		■ Tech log

Diversion:

⇨ Select a suitable airfield.
⇨ Draw track on chart:
  • Start at an identifiable point a little way ahead of present position.
  • Consider terrain/altitude.
⇨ Estimate:
  • Heading.
  • Time.
⇨ ATC.

Uncertain of position:

⇨ Fly the aeroplane.
⇨ Synchronize DI with compass.
⇨ Orientate heading and chart.
⇨ Mark estimated DR position.
⇨ Attempt to establish position.

  • After 15 minutes or so, you are lost!

Action when lost:

⇨ Fly the aeroplane.
⇨ ATC 'pan' call, Squawk 7700.

If ATC help is unavailable:
⇨ Fly a cardinal heading to an identifiable line feature.
⇨ Fly along the feature until your position is fixed.

→ Precautionary landing if necessary.

AIRMANSHIP	ENGINE HANDLING
Suitability of weather – go/no go **Lookout** Safety altitude	Normal Fuel management

PPL Exercise 18B: Low-Level Navigation

Aim: To operate safely at a low level, if forced to do so.

(Pre-) Descent

> ✈ FREDA
> ⇨ Descend to 600ft agl.

Low-Level Navigation

> *Advantages*
> • Contour and relief more apparent.
> *Disadvantages*
> • Reduced visual range.
> • Reduced radio and radio nav. beacon range.

Wind Effects

> Note:
> ▪ Turbulence – increases nearer to ground (depends on wind strength).
> ▪ Speed is more apparent.
> ▪ Increase/decrease of ground speed into/downwind.
> ▪ Crosswind drift is more apparent.

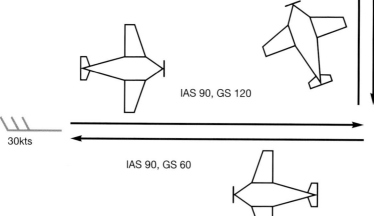

IAS 90, GS 120

30kts

IAS 90, GS 60

> ▪ Effect of drift in turns
>   ✈ especially when orbiting.

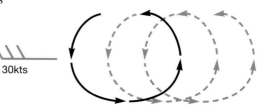

30kts

Continuous rate one turn

Low Visibility Navigation

- Low speed cruise, 70 to 75kts:
  - ☛ more time to react and navigate.
- 10° flap:
  - ☛ better forward visibility.

Bad Weather Circuit

✈ Continuous turns to downwind and finals.

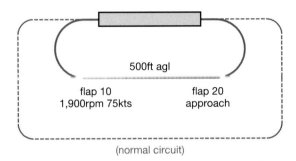

flap 10
1,900rpm 75kts

500ft agl

flap 20
approach

(normal circuit)

✈ Tight downwind to keep runway in view.

Low-Flying Regulations

- *An aircraft shall not fly closer than 500ft to any person, vessel, vehicle or structure.*
- *An aircraft shall not fly over a congested area below:*
  - *1) such a height as would enable it to land clear in the event of an engine failure;*
  - *2) a height of 1,500ft above the highest fixed object within 2,000ft.*

Exceptions:
    Take-off and landing within airspace normally used for the purpose.
    To save a life.
    Flight in accordance with the special VFR clearance.
    Organized flying displays or air racing.

AIRMANSHIP	ENGINE HANDLING
Lookout (military flights) Conspicuity – lights and transponder Obstacles/ground elevation – map Low-flying rules	Normal

PPL Exercise 18C1: Radio Nav. – ADF

Aim: To be able to fix position and home to a beacon in VMC using the ADF.

Navigational Aids

Non-directional beacon: Produces a uniform signal.

Automatic direction finder: Looks for the direction of the signal.

Relative bearing indicator (RBI): Indicates the bearing of the signal relative to the aircraft nose.

→ Use with DI.

- Fixed card – indicates the relative bearing to the aircraft nose only.
- Adjustable card – allows the compass card to be manually synchronized with the DI.

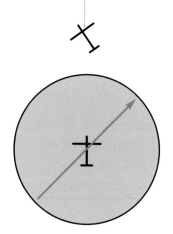

Radio magnetic indicator (RMI): Combined RBI+DI – card moves automatically as the aircraft heading changes.

Homing

⇨ Orientate to track
    ↻ Needle falls to the right   ⇨ go right.
    ↻ Needle falls to the left   ⇨ go left.
⇨ Wind drift heading (when on track).

→ Needle *always* shows the way to turn.

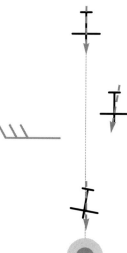

Position Fix

Find bearing:
    1. heading + relative bearing (−360).
or: 2. compare the RBI needle angular position to the centreline of the
     diagram, then add or subtract from:

⇧ heading or
⇩ reciprocal

of DI as indicated.

Repeat: Two position lines are needed for a fix.

    DI show aircraft heading 270°

NDB#1 bears 300°
☛ Reciprocal 120°

NDB#2 bear 040°
☛ Reciprocal 220°

SELECT.	IDENTIFY.	DISPLAY.
frequency	morse ident.	compass card

PPL Exercise 18C2: Radio Nav. – VOR

Aim: To be able to navigate in VMC using VHF omnidirectional range (VOR) beacons.

Navigational Aids

VHF omnidirectional range beacon: Produces a positional signal that varies with the bearing from the beacon:
- ☛ Defines a position line;
- ⇧ Sensitivity close to beacon.

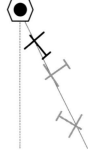

Omni bearing indicator (OBI)

✈ Course deviation indicator indicates an angular deviation from the selected position line *irrespective of heading*.

✈ Five dot display, 2° per dot

✈ Omni bearing selector (0135) selects the required course (track).

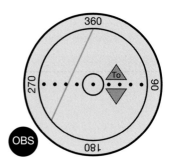

Position Fix

Find bearing: Rotate OBS until CDI centres with a *'from'* indication.

Repeat: Two position lines needed for a fix.

Bearing from VOR#1 – 120°

Bearing from VOR#2 – 220°

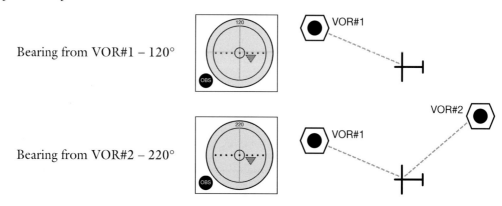

Tracking

To
- ⇨ Set OBS to required track.
- ⇨ Orientate to track
  - ➲ Needle falls to the right ⇨ go right.
  - ➲ Needle falls to the left ⇨ go left.
- ⇨ Wind drift heading (when on track).

Beacon passage
- ⇨ Maintain heading through cone of silence.

From
- ⇨ Set OBS to required track.
- ⇨ Orientate to track
  - ➲ Needle falls to the right ⇨ go right.
  - ➲ Needle falls to the left ⇨ go left.
- ⇨ Wind drift heading (when on track).

✈ *Always* set OBS to desired track whether going *to* or *from* beacon.

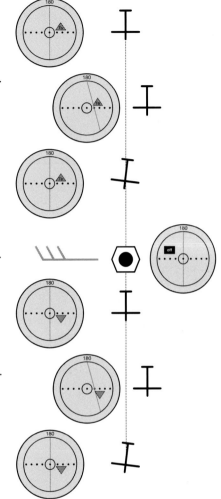

SELECT.	IDENTIFY.	DISPLAY.
frequency	morse ident.	set 0135

PPL Exercise 19: Basic Instrument Flight

Aim: To be able to fly the aircraft in instrument meteorological conditions and be able to return to VMC.

Standard instrument layout

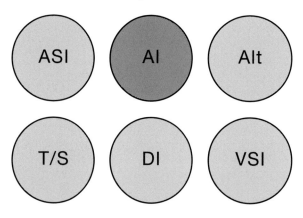

ASI: Airspeed indicator
AI: Attitude indicator
Alt: Altimeter

T/S: Turn and slip indicator
DI: Direction indicator
VSI: Vertical speed indicator

	ASI	AI	Alt	T/S	DI	VSI
Pitch information	Yes	Yes	Yes	No	No	Yes
Roll information	No	Yes	No	Yes	Yes	No

✈ Only the AI provides both pitch and roll information;
☛ it therefore becomes the 'master instrument'.

Attitude Indicator

The roll indication is given by the position of the sky pointer against the lines on the periphery of the instrument.
→ The scale is not compressed, i.e. 30° of bank = 30° of instrument movement.

The pitch indication is given by the position of the aircraft index against the pitch lines on the face of the instrument.
→ The scale is compressed, i.e. 10° of pitch causes only a small movement of the instrument.

Scan
➤ ⅔ attitude indicator: ⅓ other instruments
   (visual scan; ⅔ outside: ⅓ instruments).

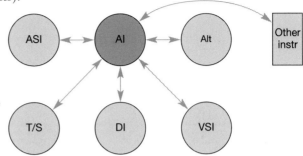

Radial scan
Centred on the attitude indicator
Scan moves out to other instruments,
and back to the attitude indicator.

Selective radial scan
Still centred on the attitude indicator, the scan concentrates more on particular instruments
at different phases of flight:

- Straight and level

  Power
  Attitude AI
  Trim

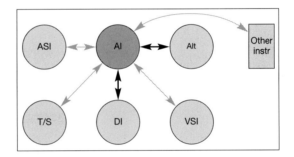

Corrections: Correct slowly to avoid overshoot.
    Heading: Bank angle = ½ heading correction.
    Altitude: Use VSI, 100/200fpm

Climbing and Descending (500fpm)

Entry: Power
Attitude
Trim

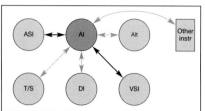

Pitch up/down using AI to achieve target airspeed (balance).

Maintaining

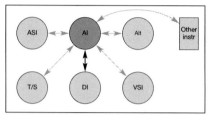

Maintain direction.

Recovery P A
A P
T T

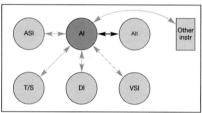

Pitch level (balance).

Turning

Entry: Bank (AI)
15° (rate one)
Balance (T/S)
Back pressure

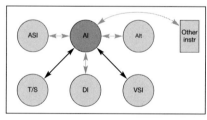

Avoid sinking.

Maintaining

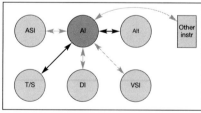

Maintain altitude.

Recovery Bank
Balance
Back pressure

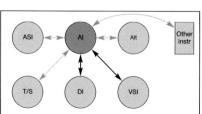

Avoid ballooning.

Cloud Breaks

> ☠ *The PPL alone is a VMC rating, and does not allow flight in IMC:*
> ⇨ If you enter IMC, return to VMC.

1. 180° Reversal

Transfer to instruments

Note heading

Cloud

Rate one level turn on
to reciprocal heading

Straight and level to exit IMC

- If this does not return you to VMC:
    - ⇨ Mayday
    - ⇨ ATC/radar assistance

2. Descend: To MSA only unless you become visual.

3. Climb: If cloud tops are low enough it may be easier to fly on top of the cloud to a safe descent position.
   ✈ Note: There is no such thing as 'VMC on top'.

AIRMANSHIP	ENGINE HANDLING

☠ Turn back, Divert, Don't leave ground
   Mayday, ATC/radar assistance
   Icing
	Carb heat

CHAPTER 2
Night Qualification

The night qualification does exactly what it says on the box: it allows you to fly at night, which for regulatory purposes starts thirty minutes after sunset, and ends thirty minutes before sunrise. To get the qualification you aren't required to do anything that you haven't already done during the PPL, except for the fact that you are now doing it at night. Indeed, the course structure mirrors that of the PPL in miniature, starting with upper air work, progressing to take-off and landing, and finishing with procedural and navigation training. There's also the solo requirement; namely five take-offs and landings (which for some inexplicable reason have to be full stop landings, not 'touch-and-goes').

The main difference with night flying is the reduction in, or alteration to, the visual cues

normally available when flying in daylight. Night-flying training is carried out in 'visual meteorological conditions'; however, visual flight rules' operation is not permitted at night, so flights are conducted under 'instrument flight rules' when outside controlled airspace, and 'Special VFR' within, irrespective of the actual meteorological conditions – however, nothing in the qualification allows the holder to enter instrument meteorological conditions unless they also hold an appropriate rating.

The qualification can be taken as an integral part of the PPL provided the minimum twenty-five hours' dual and ten hours' solo flying has already been completed; however, the average student pilot has quite enough to contend with doing their PPL training in daylight, so most people do the qualification as a separate 'add on' at a later date.

At only five hours (minimum) the qualification is the shortest of the 'associated ratings'. Apart from not having to rush back before official night when out on a day trip, flight on a clear cold night provides a dramatic and spectacular new perspective to the landscape below you.

Note: The night qualification is the JAR-FCL successor to the CAA night rating, and is exactly the same except that it doesn't entitle the holder to three hours off the IMC rating.

Night Qualification JAR-FCL Syllabus

FLIGHT TRAINING

Five hours *minimum* of which:

- Three hours' dual, including one hour night navigation.
- Five night take-offs and full stop landings.

Flight Exercises
1. Night Orientation
2. Night Circuits
3. Night Navigation
4. Night Solo (includes five take-offs and full stop landings)

Flight Test
- No flight test

GROUND TRAINING

No set hours of ground training are specified.

Ground Examination
- No ground examination.

Entry to Training

- Have completed the PPL course (may be integrated with PPL training once the twenty-five hours' dual and ten hours' solo requirements have been met).

Privileges

- Allow the holder to fly as PIC at night.

Validity

- Validity: As for the licence to which it is attached (automatically renewed when the licence is renewed).
- Three take-offs and landings in last ninety days for carriage of passengers, of which one must have been at night.

FLIGHT EXERCISES

Night Exercise 1: Night Orientation

Aim: To learn the differences of technique and perception necessary to handle an aircraft at night.

Pre-Flight Check

> ⇨ Use torch.
> ⇨ Check serviceability of aircraft lighting:
>   • external – beacon/anti-collision, landing, taxi, navigation, strobes;
>   • internal – dome, instrument, cabin.
> ⇨ Check area around aircraft.

Starting

> ⇨ Flash taxi light (landing light) three times.
> ⇨ Anti-collision beacon on.

Taxiing

> ⇨ Taxi light (landing light) on.
> ⇨ Taxi on centreline lights/markings.
> ⇨ Taxi more slowly.
> Note:
>   ▪ Speed and distance are more difficult to judge;
>   ▪ obstacles may not be easily visible.
>   ⇨ If in doubt, stop!
>   ☛ ATC/marshalling assistance.

Taxiway lighting:

centreline lights

green

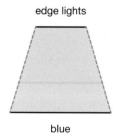

edge lights

blue

Holding Point

    ☠ Do not infringe runway.
    ⇒ Taxi light off while stationary.

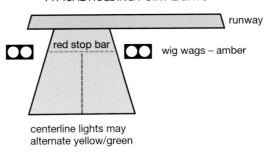

TYPICAL HOLDING POINT LIGHTS

runway

red stop bar

wig wags – amber

centerline lights may
alternate yellow/green

In flight

Normal use of Power, Attitude, Trim:

- Horizon is less apparent:
    ⇒ Use of instruments.
    ⇒ Use of peripheral vision/lateral view.

- Lighted ground features appear closer.

- Traffic avoidance:
    ⇒ Use navigation lights:

Red to red:	safe
Green to green:	safe
Red to green:	unsafe

AIRMANSHIP

Lookout – aircraft lighting
Torch/batteries backup light source

Correct use/setting of aircraft lighting
– don't dazzle other pilots

Night Exercise 2: Night Circuits

Aim: To learn to take off and land at night.

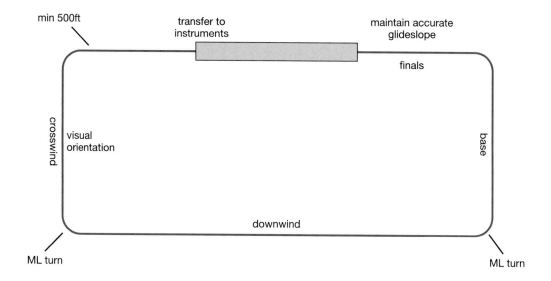

Take-Off

- Normal take-off roll
- Rotate
    ⇨ Transfer to instruments.

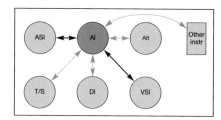

    Attitude:
        ⇨ Positive rate of climb.
        ⇨ Correct airspeed.

✈ Greater use of peripheral vision than by day;
⇨ Climb straight ahead to 500ft agl.

Circuit

- Aim to fly normal circuit:
⇨ Visual orientate on crosswind.
✈ Directional runway/approach lights may not be visible until base leg/final:
    ⇨ Use surrounding lights to orientate.

Approach

Judge approach using:

- PAPIs

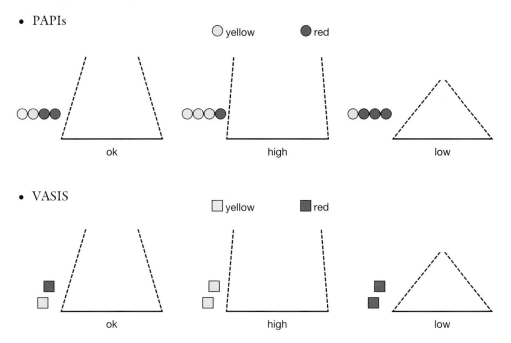

- VASIS

- Runway edge lighting perspective

Landing

✈ Avoid flaring too high;
✈ Judge flare using peripheral vision of edge lights.

AIRMANSHIP

Lookout
Accurate approach path

Anticipate change of wind direction with
height on approach

Night Exercise 3: Night Navigation

Aim: To navigate across country and join an aerodrome traffic pattern safely at night.

Planning/Pre-Flight	En route	Arrival

Weather
■ Temperature/dewpoint
■ Change of wind direction with altitude
 	
Alternates
■ En route (for diversions)
■ Destination alternates
  ✈ Availability/suitability
 	
Route
■ Use waypoints likely to be visible at night:
  – towns
  – major roads
  – lighted structures
■ Controlled airspace etc.
  ✈ hours of operation
 	
Prepare Chart
■ Make chart with colours visible under night lighting conditions (Red is not visible under red light)
 	
Complete Plog
■ Minimum safety altitude
■ Radio/nav frequencies
  ✈ hours of operation
■ Fuel calculations
  ✈ greater reserve
	Aviate
	⇨ Fly aeroplane
	⇨ Greater reliance on instruments
	⇨ Avoid accidental entry into IMC
	
	Navigate
	⇨ Maintain course
	  ✈ Ground features appear closer than they actually are
	⇨ Fly appropriate quadrantal/semi-circular altitude (IFR)
	  ✈ VFR does not exist at night
	
	even + 500 _____ odd
	270 | 0~
	360 | 089
	180 | 090
	269 | 179
	even _____ odd + 500
	
	⇨ Radio navigation
	
	Communicate
	■ Fewer ATC stations available at night
		ATC
		⇨ Weather info
		⇨ SVFR in controlled airspace
		  ✈ VFR does not exist at night
		
		Joining
		⇨ Greater use of DI/compass to orientate as runway lighting may not be visible until lined up
		
		Diversion
		⇨ Maximum use of ATC assistance
		■ Otherwise as for day

Night Emergencies

Lost/uncertain of position
- ✈ Ensure altitude > MSA:
- ⇨ Early 'Pan' call.
- ▪ Otherwise as for day.

Electrical failure
- ✈ Use of lights = greater load:
- ⇨ Shed load.
- ⇨ Divert/land ASAP?

Engine failure
- ⇨ Maintain safe airspeed.
- ⇨ Drills as for day.
- ⇨ Land with minimum safe forward speed.

Landing-area selection
- ▪ Lighted:
  - ☛ Able to see obstructions/terrain.
- ▪ Dark:
  - ☛ Fewer man-made obstructions likely.

AIRMANSHIP

Lookout   Compliance with IFR/SVFR
Awareness of nearest diversion

CHAPTER 3

Instrument Meteorological Conditions Rating

The instrument meteorological conditions rating is an exclusively British phenomenon, and as such is not valid anywhere else. It exists, of course, as a response to the unpredictability (euphemism for general dismalness) of our climate, and allows the holder to take off, land, and accept SVFR clearances in reduced visibility. More importantly it allows flight in instrument meteorological conditions, in 'class D or E' airspace, which opens up most of the UK's airports for instrument approaches: it is often thought of as a sort of mini instrument rating. However, it is not a full instrument rating, and the above privileges do not apply to 'class A' airspace – so don't expect to turn up at Heathrow in a Cessna 152 and be welcomed with open arms.

There are two main parts to the course: instrument flight, and instrument navigation. The first of these was touched on during the PPL, primarily as a way to get you back out of IMC if you blundered into it, and as a warning not to go there in the first place without the proper training. Obviously all that changes when you are training for the IMC rating – then you have to become competent at instrument flight in order to deal with the second part of the course, instrument navigation.

Some instrument navigation was covered, though at a superficial level, during the PPL, but mainly as an adjunct to VFR navigation. In the IMC course you not only have to be able to navigate in instrument flight conditions, but the syllabus is expanded and includes instrument approaches. At present, use of GPS is not approved as a primary means of navigation and so is not included in the syllabus.

At fifteen hours' flight time (minimum) the IMC is the longest of the 'associated' ratings, and not without good reason. Single pilot operation in IMC is a particularly demanding discipline, and the changeability of our weather and the complexity of UK airspace make it even more challenging. Currency is especially important, and a pilot who has not maintained currency, or practised instrument flying recently, should not assume they are safe to launch into IMC just because their rating is still valid.

Another point worth making is that just about all light single-engine aircraft (and even many light twins) are not equipped or certified for operation in icing conditions, i.e. the presence of visible moisture (cloud, rain, and so on) and a temperature of 0°C or less. Obviously such conditions can occur over large parts of the UK for considerable periods of the year, and all pilots should be aware of the dangers of ice accretion on an airframe. The possession of an IMC rating does not exempt you from the laws of aerodynamics.

Despite the comments above, many pilots use their IMC rating very effectively to increase their available range of flight conditions, and their ability to get from A to B. The training is very worthwhile, and there are obvious safety advantages to being able to cope with instrument conditions. However, the IMC rating, more than any other, requires good sense and sound judgement (qualities that used to be known as 'airmanship') if you are to be able to exercise its privileges safely.

IMC – CAA Syllabus
Instrument Meteorological Conditions Rating

FLIGHT TRAINING

Fifteen hours *minimum* [1,2], of which:
- Ten hours by sole reference to instruments

Flight Exercises

Instrument flight:
- Full panel
- Limited panel

Instrument navigation
- ADF
- VOR
- DME
- Approach and let down procedures
- Approaches: NDB/locator, ILS and radar approaches
- Holding
- Bad weather circuits
- (Asymmetric instrument flying[3])

Flight Test[4]
1. Full Panel Instrument Flying
2. Limited Panel Instrument Flying
3. Radio Navigation Aids
4. Approach and Let Down
5. Bad Weather Circuits
6. (Asymmetric Instrument Flying[3])

[1] Two hours may be on an approved flight sim.
[2] If night rated 12 hours, of which 8 hours by sole ref to instruments.
[3] If training to be conducted on a multi-engine aircraft.
[4] Failure of any section requires complete retest.

Entry to Training

- Twenty-five hours since application for PPL[5] of which:
    Ten hours PIC
        – Five hours solo cross-country
- FRTO licence

[5] Which may include the 15 hours of the course.

GROUND TRAINING

Twenty hours *minimum.*

Subjects

- Physiological factors
- Flight instruments/radio aids
- Aeronautical information services/ATC
- Flight planning
- Air law and privileges

Ground Examination
(Multi-choice, passmark 75%)
Covers the subjects above and may include questions drawn from the PPL syllabus.

Privileges (UK, CI and IoM only)

Allow the holder to fly as PIC:

- Out of sight of the surface.
- In a control zone on a SVFR clearance in a flight visibility of less than 10km but not less than 3km.
- In IMC outside controlled airspace, and in class D or E airspace.
- During take-off and landing with a flight visibility below cloud of not less than 1,800m.

Validity

- Validity: Twenty-five months
- Renewal flight test [6]
- Log-book evidence of an approach to minima, go around and missed approach
  OR: Two approaches during renewal flight test.

[6] Items 2, 4, 5 (and 6) of initial test.

IMC Exercise 1: Instrument Flying (Full Panel)

Aim: To be able to fly the aircraft in instrument meteorological conditions.

Standard instrument layout

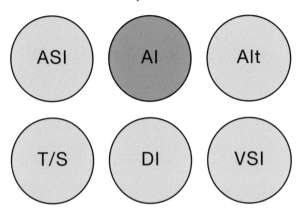

ASI: Airspeed indicator
AI: Attitude indicator
Alt: Altimeter

T/S: Turn and slip indicator
DI: Direction indicator
VSI: Vertical speed indicator

	ASI	AI	Alt	T/S	DI	VSI
Pitch information	Yes	Yes	Yes	No	No	Yes
Roll information	No	Yes	No	Yes	Yes	No

➤ Only the AI provides both pitch and roll information;
☛ It therefore becomes the 'master instrument'.

Attitude Indicator

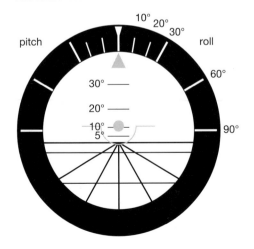

The roll indication is given by the position of the sky pointer against the lines on the periphery of the instrument.
➤ The scale is not compressed, i.e. 30° of bank = 30° of instrument movement.

The pitch indication is given by the position of the aircraft index against the pitch lines on the face of the instrument.
➤ The scale is compressed, i.e. 10° of pitch causes only a small movement of the instrument.

Scan

➜ ⅔ attitude indicator: ⅓ other instruments
(visual scan, ⅔ outside: ⅓ instruments).

Radial Scan

Centred on the attitude indicator:
The scan moves out to other
instruments, and back to the
attitude indicator.

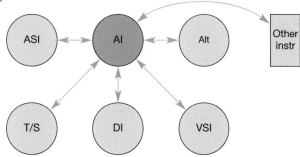

Selective Radial Scan

Still centred on the attitude indicator, the scan concentrates more on particular instruments
at different phases of flight:

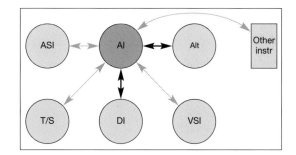

- **Straight and Level**
  Power
  Attitude (AI)
  Trim

Corrections:	Correct slowly to avoid overshoot.
Heading:	Bank angle = ½ heading correction.
Altitude:	Use VSI, 100/200fpm.

Ice Encounter

➜ When in IMC the cruise check should now include
a visual inspection of the airframe for ice build-up.

■ If ice is encountered:
  ⇨ Turn back.
  ⇨ Descend below icing level or into clear air.
    ☠ Check MSA.
  ⇨ Climb to clear air above.
    ➜ Check controlled airspace.

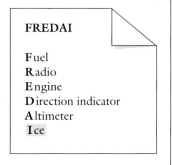

FREDAI

Fuel
Radio
Engine
Direction indicator
Altimeter
Ice

Climbing and Descending (500fpm)

Entry:	Power Attitude Trim	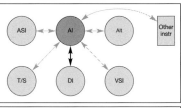		Pitch up/down using AI to achieve target airspeed (balance).
Maintaining		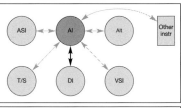		Maintain direction.
Recovery	P A A P T T	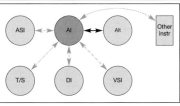		Pitch level (balance).

Turning

Entry:	Bank (AI) 15° (rate one) Balance (T/S) Back pressure	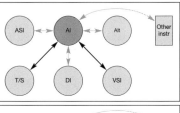		Avoid sinking.
Maintaining				Maintain altitude.
Recovery	B B B	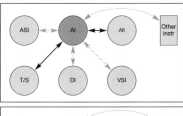		Avoid ballooning.

AIRMANSHIP	FREDA I	**ENGINE HANDLING**
Radar service Min safe alt		Carb heat

IMC Exercise 2: Instrument Flying (Limited Panel)

Aim: To be able to fly the aircraft and recover from unusual attitudes, in instrument meteorological conditions on a limited panel.

Available Instruments Following Suction Failure

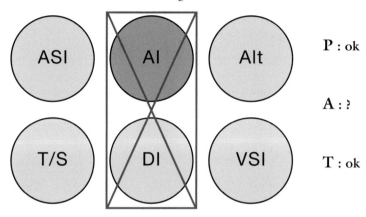

P : ok

A : ?

T : ok

	ASI	AI	Alt	T/S	DI	VSI
Pitch information	Yes	Yes	Yes	No	No	Yes
Roll information	No	Yes	No	Yes	Yes	No

Scan

No single instrument provides both pitch and roll information.
⇨ ASI and turn co-ordinator become the 'master instrument':
    ASI ☛ pitch   when compared to rpm.
    T/S ☛ bank   provided slip ball centralized.

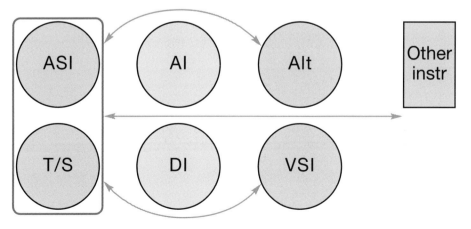

Straight and Level

Power.
Attitude – ASI + T/S.
Trim.

Climbing

Entry
Power – allow aircraft to pitch up.
Attitude – small pitch changes to give correct IAS.
Trim.

Recovery
Attitude – use VSI lag – Pitch down, as soon as VSI moves, check pitch input.
Power – when airspeed returns, reset power.
Trim.

Descending (500fpm)

Entry
Power – allow aircraft to pitch down.
Attitude – small pitch changes to give correct IAS.
Do not trim.

Recovery
Power – reset.
Attitude – should find its own level, as no trim change was made.

Turning

Entry
Bank – T/S (rate one).
Balance – T/S.
Back pressure – VSI.

Timing
30° = 10 seconds.
10° = 3 seconds.
(Work out timing using any convenient compass rose.)

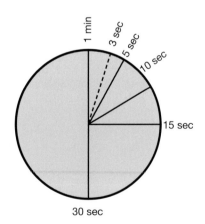

➜ Start timing at the start of rolling into the turn.
➜ Maintain rate one turn until time has elapsed and begin roll out.

Recovery
Check compass and adjust.

Unusual Attitudes

1. Nose down – airspeed increasing.
   ⇨ Wings level.
   ⇨ Pitch up gently, until VSI just starts to indicate a decreased rate of descent.
   ⇨ Power when ASI normal.

2. Nose up – airspeed low/decreasing.
   ⇨ Wings level.
   ⇨ Pitch down gently, until VSI just starts to indicate a decreased rate of climb.
   ⇨ Power when ASI normal.

3. Level – airspeed high/decreasing or low/increasing – this is a trick!
   ⇨ Wings level.
   ⇨ Power when ASI normal.

AIRMANSHIP	ENGINE HANDLING
Mayday	Carb heat
FREDA I Radar service Min safe alt	

IMC Exercise 3: ADF

Aim: To be able to navigate using the automatic direction finding (ADF) equipment.

Navigational Aids

Non-directional beacon: Produces a uniform signal.

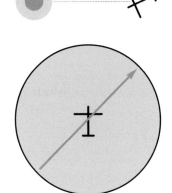

Automatic direction finder: Looks for direction of signal.

Relative bearing indicator (RBI): Indicates bearing of signal relative to aircraft nose.

→ Use with DI.

- Fixed card – indicates relative bearing to aircraft nose only.
- Adjustable card – allows compass card to be manually synchronized with the DI.

Radio magnetic indicator (RMI): Combined RBI + DI – card moves automatically as aircraft heading changes.

Position Fix

Find bearing:
1. Heading + relative bearing (−360).
or: 2. Compare RBI needle angular position to **centreline** of diagram, then add or subtract from:

⇧ Heading or
⇩ Reciprocal
of DI as indicated.

Repeat: Two position lines are needed for a fix:

DI shows aircraft heading 270°

NDB#1 bears 300°
☞ reciprocal 120°

NDB#2 bears 040°
☞ reciprocal 220°

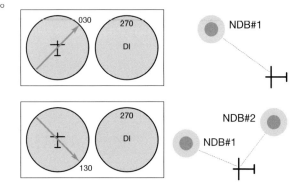

Tracking

✈ Needle *always* shows way to turn.

To
⇨ Orientate to track:
➲ Needle falls to right ⇨ go right.
➲ Needle falls to left ⇨ go left.
⇨ Wind drift heading
(when on track)

Beacon passage
✈ Sensitivity increased close to beacon:
⇨ Maintain heading as needle turns.

From
⇨ Orientate to track:
➲ Needle falls to right ⇨ go right.
➲ Needle falls to left ⇨ go left.
OR:
➲ Tail of needle right ⇨ go left.
➲ Trail of needle left ⇨ go right.
⇨ Wind drift heading
(when on track).

Intercept

⇨ Orientate to track.
✈ Needle *always* shows way to turn.   30° intercept*

10nm

60° intercept*

20nm

90° intercept*

* reduce intercept angle as track comes in.

SELECT.   IDENTIFY.   DISPLAY.

IMC Exercise 4: VOR

Aim: To be able to navigate using VHF omnidirectional range (VOR) beacons.

Navigational Aids

VHF Omnidirectional Range Beacon
    Produces positional signal that
    varies with bearing from beacon.
        ☞ Defines a position line.
        Increased sensitivity close
        to beacon.

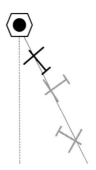

Omni-Bearing Indicator (OBI)
    ✦ Course deviation indicator (CDI) indicates angular deviation from selected position
        line *irrespective of heading.*

    ✦ Five-dot display,
        2° per dot.

    ✦ Omni-bearing selector (OBS) selects required
        course (track).

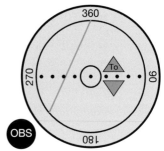

Position Fix

Find bearing: Rotate OBS until CDI centres with a *from* indication.

Repeat: Two position lines are needed for a fix.

bearing from VOR#1 – 120°

bearing from VOR#2 – 220°

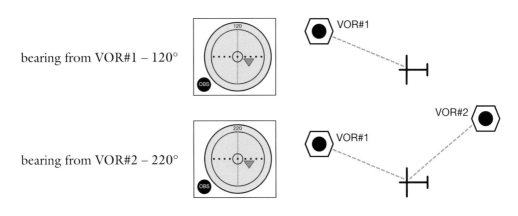

Tracking

To
- ⇨ Set OBS to required track.
- ⇨ Orientate to track:
  - ➲ Needle falls to right   ⇨ go right.
  - ➲ Needle falls to left   ⇨ go left.
- ⇨ Wind drift heading
  (when on track).

Beacon passage
- ⇨ Maintain heading through cone of silence.

From
- ⇨ Set OBS to required track.
- ⇨ Orientate to track:
  - ➲ Needle falls to right   ⇨ go right.
  - ➲ Needle falls to left   ⇨ go left.
- ⇨ Wind drift heading
  (when on track).

✦ *Always* set OBS to desired track
whether going *to* or *from* beacon.

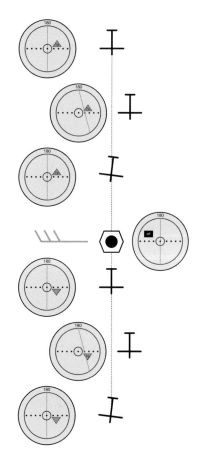

Intercept

      Orientate to track.

               30° intercept*

               10nm

               60° intercept*

               20nm

               90° intercept*

     * reduce angle of intercept as track comes in.

| SELECT. | IDENTIFY. | DISPLAY. |

IMC Exercise 5: DME

Aim: To understand the use of distance measuring equipment (DME).

DME

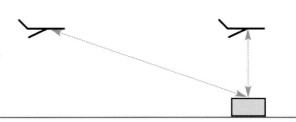

    Measures the distance between
the aircraft and station.

✦ Slant range – therefore more
accurate at greater range.

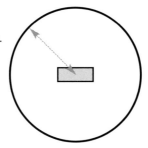

✦ Defines a circular position line.

✦ Readout to ⅒ mile
(one decimal place).

DME Arc

✦ Aim is to fly an arc at a constant DME distance:
    ⇨ Orientate at 90° to DME.
        ➲ DME distance less than required:
           ⇨ Maintain heading.
        ➲ DME distance more than required:
           ⇨ Turn towards DME.

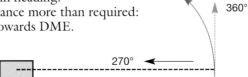

Position Fix

- ◆ Positional ambiguity with only two DMEs.

- ◆ Three DMEs required for fix.

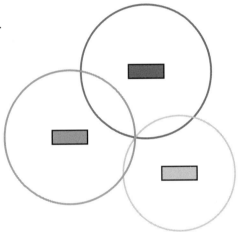

- ✈ Best used in conjunction with a beacon
  giving a linear position line (e.g. VOR/DME).

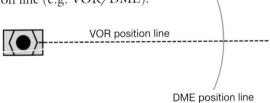

VOR position line

DME position line

SELECT.   IDENTIFY.   DISPLAY.

IMC Exercise 6: Approach Procedures

Aim: To be able to fly a procedural approach.

In practical terms a procedural approach consists of the following elements:

- Tracking towards the initial approach fix (usually a beacon, NDB/VOR).
- An intermediate phase in which the aircraft is flown outbound from the initial approach fix and manoeuvred on to the final approach track (usually via a base or procedure turn).
- Final approach from the final approach fix to landing, or go around.
- Missed approach.

➤ Determine:
  - Intercept heading
  - Drift heading
  - Rate of descent

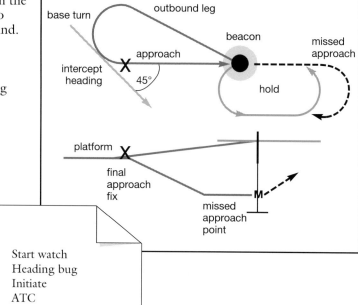

Checks at the Beacon

TTTT

Time	Start watch
Twist	Heading bug
Turn	Initiate
Talk	ATC

Procedure Turn

➤ The 45° outbound leg is a track:
  ⇨ Adjust heading and timing for wind drift.

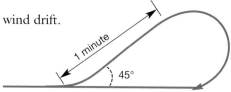

AIRMANSHIP	**ENGINE HANDLING**
Minima (approach ban)	Carb heat – white arc
Sector safe altitude	

Determination of Minima

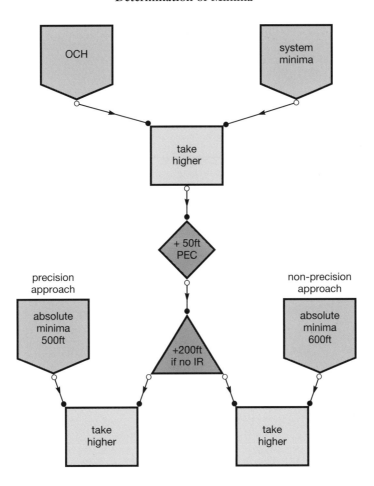

Precision Approaches

♦ Continuous glideslope guidance:
  ☛ decision height;
  ↗ generally aligned with runway.

- Instrument landing system (ILS)
- Precision approach radar (PAR)

Non-Precision Approaches

♦ No glideslope guidance (step-down fix):
  ☛ minimum descent height;
  ↗ approach may be offset.

- Localizer only approach
- Surveillance radar approach (SRA)
- VOR approach
- NDB/locator approach
- VHF direction finder approach
  (QDM or QGH)

IMC Exercise 7: Instrument Approaches 1 – NDB

Aim: To be able to fly a NDB/locator approach.

Lateral guidance
⇨ Track the ADF needle.

Vertical profile (non-precision)
- With DME ⇨ Descent is commenced at a DME distance, and monitored by using the height against the DME distance table on approach plate.
- Without DME ⇨ Descent points are determined by a fix or by timing from a fix.

✦ You may only descend if 'established' – within ±5° of the inbound track.

✦ Stepdown fixes are *minimum* heights
⇨ If the stepdown height is reached before the fix position, fly level and resume descent at the fix.

✦ The approach ends at the missed approach point, which may be a DME position or be determined by a fix or by timing from a fix.

Approach Procedure

Intercept inbound track:
⇨ 85/90kts (stay at clean cruise speed in a light single).
⇨ Track on ADF:
Call 'established' when within ±5° of inbound track.

Final approach fix:
⇨ Start timing.

Descent point:
⇨ Start descent.
⇨ Aim: to descend slightly below profile (except for stepdown fixes).

Minimum descent height
- If visual ⇨ Land – landing flap – normal approach speed.
- If not visual ⇨ Fly level – continue inbound to missed approach point – land if visual reference achieved.

Missed approach point
If visual reference is not achieved ⇨ Go around – missed approach.

⚕ On a non-precision approach you must not descend below the minimum descent height.

IMC Exercise 7: Instrument Approaches 2 – ILS

Aim: To be able to fly an ILS approach.

Instrument landing system
- Localizer – horizontal position.
- Glideslope – vertical position.

Lateral guidance
⇨ Track the localizer needle (CDI):
✦ Indicates angular deviation from localizer irrespective of heading.

Vertical profile
⇨ Follow the glideslope needle:
✦ Indicates angular deviation from glideslope irrespective of attitude.

ILS Meter (OBI)
✦ Five-dot display

| Localizer | ½° per dot. |
| Glideslope | 0.15° per dot. |

✦ Omni bearing selector has no function.

The Approach

Intercept inbound track:
⇨ 90kts.
⇨ Track on localizer:
  Call 'established' when less than half scale deflection.

Final approach fix.
⇨ Start timing.

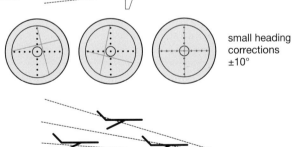

small heading corrections ±10°

Glideslope intercept:
⇨ Start descent;
⇨ 1,900rpm ±100rpm per 10kts hwc/twc;
⇨ follow glideslope needle.

Decision height:
➲ If visual   ⇨ Land – landing flap – normal approach speed.
➲ If not visual   ⇨ Go around – missed approach.

✦ On a precision approach, a 'Go-around' initiated at decision height will take the aircraft slightly below decision height (as the descent cannot be arrested instantaneously) – this is allowed for.

Localizer Only Approach

Lateral guidance
⇨ Track the ILS localizer needle (as for an ILS approach).

Vertical profile (non-precision – as for an NDB approach)
- With DME   ⇨ Descent is commenced at a DME distance, and monitored by height against the DME distance table on approach plate.
- Without DME   ⇨ Descent points are determined by a fix, or by timing from a fix.

⇨ Descent to minimum descent height.
⇨ Go around at the missed approach point if not visual.

VOR Approach

- Inbound tracking on a VOR radial.

Lateral guidance
⇨ Track the VOR course deviation indicator (which is, of course, the same as the ILS localizer needle).

Vertical profile (non-precision – as for an NDB approach).

Note:
✈ Omni bearing selector is now functional and the CDI must be set to the correct course.
✈ Omni bearing indicator display represents 2° per dot (versus ½° per dot for ILS);
  ☞ CDI is less sensitive.

IMC Exercise 7: Instrument Approaches 3

Aim: To be able to fly an ATC controlled approach.

Radar Approaches

Surveillance Radar Approach (SRA)
- ATC determines the aircraft's lateral position using radar.

Precision Approach Radar (PAR)
- In addition to the above, the controller has a vertically scanning radar and is able to monitor the aircraft's vertical position in relation to the glideslope.

Lateral guidance
⇨ Fly headings passed by ATC.

Vertical profile
⇨ Descent is commenced when instructed by ATC.
- SRA   ⇨ ATC will pass the expected height at given distances; it is up to the pilot to adjust the rate of descent to achieve the correct heights.
⇨ Non-precision approach – the approach ends at minimum descent height/missed approach point.
- PAR   ⇨ ATC will instruct the pilot to increase or decrease the rate of descent to achieve glideslope.
⇨ Precision approach – approach ends at decision height.

VDF Approaches

Lateral guidance
⇨ Home to station using QDMs passed by ATC:
↺ QDM increases   ⇨ right heading adjustment.
(aircraft is drifting left of track)
↺ QDM decreases   ⇨ left heading adjustment.
(aircraft is drifting right of track)

Vertical profile
✈ Initial fix obtained when aircraft homes to overhead station.
⇨ Descent profile is determined by timing from this point.

QGH approach – as VDF, but ATC interprets drift and heading corrections.

AIRMANSHIP	ENGINE HANDLING
Minima (approach ban)	Carb heat – white arc
Ident locator during approach	

IMC Exercise 8: Holding

Aim: To be able to fly the holding pattern accurately.

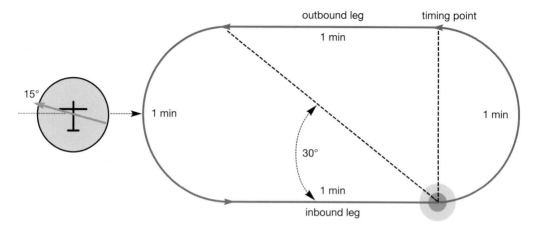

✈ Aim to achieve a 1min inbound leg within ±5° of track.

Correction for crosswind component:

✈ Apply 3× drift on outbound leg:
- Max drift (*see* box);
- *or* use 'whizzwheel'.

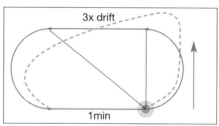

Correction for head/tailwind component:

✈ ±1sec per knot head/tailwind component from timing point on outbound leg.

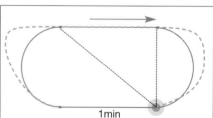

Max drift

Max drift = $\dfrac{\text{w/s} \times 60}{\text{a/s}}$

✈ most light singles cruise at about 90kts, so:

max drift = w/s × ⁶⁰⁄₉₀

= w/s × ⅔

⇨ Then multiply the max drift by a component for 'angle off' to get the actual drift:

angle off	component
30°	0.5
45°	0.7
60°	0.9

Entry to The Hold

→ Entry depends on the
aircraft's heading inbound
to the holding fix.

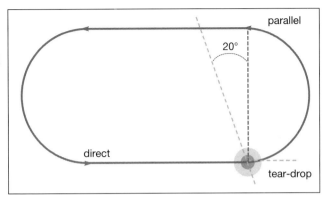

Direct:

- At the beacon the aircraft is turned directly
into the hold.

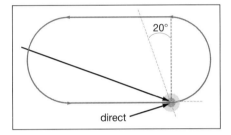

Parallel:

- At the beacon the aircraft is turned outbound
parallel to the inbound track, then turned
back to the beacon into the holding pattern.

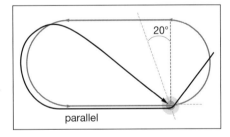

Tear-drop:

- At the beacon the aircraft is turned to
cross the pattern at 30° to the inbound
track, then turned in the direction of the
hold to intercept the inbound track.

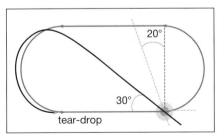

AIRMANSHIP	**R/T**
TTTT Min holding level/alt	'Beacon joining' 'Taking up the hold' 'Beacon outbound'

IMC Exercise 9: Bad Weather Circuit – Circle to Land

Aim: To be able to fly a bad weather circuit and circle to land.

Low Vis/Bad Weather Circuit

    1,900rpm, 10° flap, 75kts

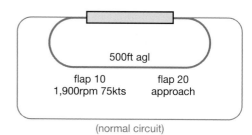

(normal circuit)

✈ Continuous turns to downwind and finals.

✈ Tight downwind to keep runway in view.

Circle to Land

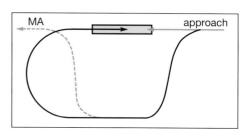

• Instrument runway is not the same as the landing runway.

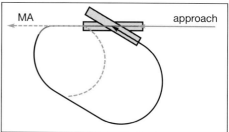

• Runway became visual too late to land.

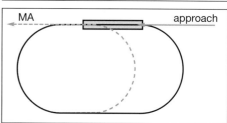

✈ **The missed approach procedure is always that appropriate to the original instrument approach.**

AIRMANSHIP	ENGINE HANDLING
Maintain visual contact or GA Min circling height	Smooth handling Carb heat

CHAPTER 4
Multi-Engine Piston Rating

Multi-engine aircraft come in a number of shapes and sizes, however this book deals with the wing-mounted twin configuration, as this has become very much the standard design for the propeller aircraft that readers of this book are likely to encounter. The advantages of this design are engineering simplicity, the mounting of the engines near the longitudinal C of G, and the ease of detection of an engine failure. The main disadvantage is that of reduced controllability due to asymmetric thrust following an engine failure.

The multi-engine piston (MEP) rating divides naturally into two sections: 'type conversion' and 'asymmetric flight', and each of these sections then further subdivides into upper air work and circuits. The first of these sections, the 'type conversion', is concerned with the operation of the aircraft with both engines working, and here the general principals of operation are the same as for a single. So, for example, to start a climb the pilot must set power, select a suitable attitude to achieve the appropriate airspeed, and trim the aircraft (the 'power-attitude-trim' procedure familiar to any single-engine pilot).

Having said that, a twin is generally larger and more complex, and the extent to which the type conversion represents a step change for the student pilot will depend on the complexity of the single-engine aircraft that he or she has already flown. A student who has only experienced fixed undercarriage and fixed pitch propeller aircraft will, as part of their training, almost certainly have to come to terms with retractable undercarriages and variable pitch props (*see* Chapter 5, Differences), and while this presents no great problem, it is the author's experience that a pilot with this sort of background will generally take a little longer than the two-and-a-half hours' maximum two-engine time allowed if the rating is to be completed in the minimum six hours total. It follows that if a pilot is already familiar with these refinements he will find the conversion easier, so if the prospective twin student has the opportunity to fly more complex single-engine aircraft, this may prove valuable.

The other point worth making is that twins usually have greater mass and, therefore, greater inertia than a single. On the one hand this means greater stability, but on the other, more time, effort and airspace is required to stop the aircraft doing whatever it's doing and make it do something else instead. Twins also tend to have better performance (in terms of speed and rates of climb and so on), so it's much easier to bust your altitude, infringe controlled airspace, or end up in that 'Cb' that seemed so far away just a few minutes ago. Taken together, what this adds up to, is that more anticipation and appreciation of energy management is required to fly a twin, and also, perhaps, a more procedural mind set.

The second half of the twin rating 'asymmetric flight' concerns the ability to deal with an engine failure and then maintain flight on the remaining engine. This ability to suffer an engine failure and still return safely to an airfield is, of course, one of the main advantages of multi-engine aircraft (though there is an ongoing debate about the relative reliability of multiple-piston-engine aircraft versus single-engine turbine machines). Flight on a single engine (in a multi-engine aircraft) will be very different to anything the student has experienced before, because engine failure turns a high-performance aircraft into a heavy, low-performance aircraft. This is because although available thrust has only been reduced by half, the displaced thrust axis and increased drag means performance can reduce to as little as 10 per cent of the all-engines' figure.

In terms of hours, the 'twin rating' is relatively short, but is both challenging and fun, and allows the PPL holder to go further, faster and to carry more payload.

MEP: JAR-FCL Syllabus
Multi-Engine Piston Class Rating

FLIGHT TRAINING
Six hours *minimum* (+ test), of which:

- 2½ hr normal
- 3½ hr asymmetric

Flight Exercises

F1. Initial Type Conversation
F2. Circuits
F3. Introduction to Asymmetric Flight
F4. Critical and Safety Speeds
F5. Asymmetric Circuits
F6. Asymmetric Performance and Circuits

MEP Skill Test
1. Pre-Flight
2. General Handling
3. Emergency Procedures
4. Circuit
5. Navigation
6. Type/Class Specific Procedures
   ☛ Asymmetric Flight

GROUND TRAINING
Seven hours *minimum*.

Lessons

- LB1 Aeroplane and Engine Systems
- LB2 Variable Pitch Propellers and feathering
- LB3 Principles of Multi-Engined Flight
- LB4 Minimum Control and Safety Speeds
- LB5 Weight and Balance
- LB6 Effect of Engine Failure on Systems and Performance
- LB7 Weight and Performance

Ground Examination (Multi-choice, passmark 75%)
40 (min) Multi-choice questions of which:
- 60% general MEP operation
- 40% type specific

Entry to Training

- Seventy hours PIC

Privileges

- Fly MEP aeroplanes included within the 'class'
- Fly a different type within the class with only a minimum of additional familiarization training

Currency

- ✔ Validity: One year
- ✔ Proficiency check [1] in last three months of validity
- ✔ Ten route sectors [2] *or* one route sector with examiner[1]
- ✔ Three take-offs and landings in last ninety days (in MEP a/c) for carriage of passengers

[1] May be combined in same flight.
[2] Route sector = T/o, 15min cruise and ldg.

FLIGHT EXERCISES

MEP Exercise F1: Initial Type Conversion

Aim: To observe the differences in multi-engine aircraft handling, and to learn the use of controls and systems, to explore stall performance and become familiar with the emergency checklist.

Taxiing
    Increased power to move off.
    More room/braking needed to stop.
    ✈ Grass to concrete transition at 90°

Take-off
    Throttle: t/o, RPM: Max, MIX: rich
    Rotate
    ☛ Positive rate of climb
        ⇨ Brakes on/off
        ⇨ Gear up
        ⇨ Set climb power
            (MFP RPM MIX)
        ⇨ At 1,000ft fuel pumps off
            (one at a time)

Climb
    Power (MIX RPM MFP)
    Attitude
    Trim

    ✈ MFP reduces by approx 1in
    per 1,000ft
        ⇨ Reset MFP
    ✈ Anticipate level-off

Level off
    Attitude – allow aircraft to accelerate
    Power (MFP RPM MIX)
    Trim progressive during acceleration
    (cowl flaps)

Turns
    Note: greater control loads

Systems
    ⇨ Gear – lower/raise
    ⇨ Flaps – lower/raise
    Note:
        ▪ Limiting speed
        ▪ Trim changes

Descending
    Power (MFP RPM MIX)
    Attitude
    Trim

    ✈ MFP increases by approx 1in
    per 1,000ft
        ⇨ Reset MFP
    ✈ Anticipate level-off

Engine Controls

✈ Increase power
    ⇨ right to left

✈ Decrease power
    ⇨ left to right

MFP gauge	RPM gauge	fuel flow gauge
throttle (black)	propeller lever (blue)	mixture control (red)

✈ Cowl flaps control the cooling airflow around the outside of the engine, and are used in conjunction with the cylinder head temperature (CHT) gauge.
    Speed low, power high ☛ high CHT ⇨ open cowl flaps.
    Speed high, power low ☛ low CHT ⇨ close cowl flaps.

Emergency Checklist

Memory items versus reference to checklist (*see* Appendix I & II).

Stalling

Entry	During	Recovery

HASELL
Fuel pumps on
Main tanks selected
MIX: rich
RPM: top of green arc
 	
1. Clean
   Power: idle
   Gear: up
   Flap: up
 	
2. Final approach
   Power: low
   Gear: down
   Flap: full
 	
3. Final turn
   Power: low
   Gear: down
   Flap: intermediate
	Note:
	  ■ Start altitude
	  ■ Recovery altitude
	
	☞ More height required
	   to recover than in a
	   single-engined aircraft
		Full Power
		  ■ Look for 'asymmetric
		    pick-up' – one engine
		    increasing power more
		    quickly than the other.
		  ☠ Close both throttles if
		    one engine fails during
		    recovery.
		
		Stick Forward
		
		Opposite rudder
		          – Arrest yaw
		
		⇨ Recover to climb

Steep Turns

     45–60° left/right
         ➜ *No* increase in power necessary.
         ➜ Strong back pressure required.

AIRMANSHIP	**ENGINE HANDLING**
Lookout Increased performance ⇨ Greater anticipation HASELL	Smooth operation Mixture Cowl flaps Caution asymmetric pick-up

MEP Exercise F2: Circuits

Aim: To learn to take off and land in a multi-engine aircraft with both engines operating.

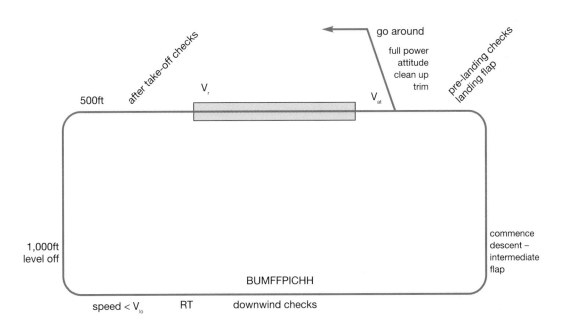

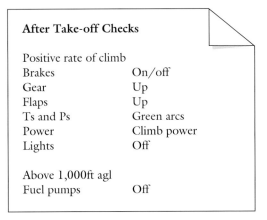

After Take-off Checks

Positive rate of climb	
Brakes	On/off
Gear	Up
Flaps	Up
Ts and Ps	Green arcs
Power	Climb power
Lights	Off
Above 1,000ft agl	
Fuel pumps	Off

BUMFFPICHH

Brakes	Off
Undercarriage	Down
Mixture	Rich
Fuel	Sufficient/pumps on
Flaps	As required
Pitch	Fully fine/max rpm
Instruments	Set
Cowl Flaps	Open
Hatches	Secure
Harnesses	Secure

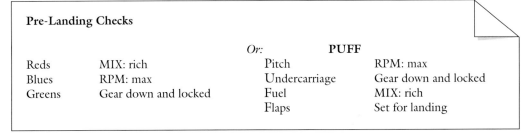

Pre-Landing Checks

Reds	MIX: rich	*Or:*	**PUFF**
Blues	RPM: max	Pitch	RPM: max
Greens	Gear down and locked	Undercarriage	Gear down and locked
		Fuel	MIX: rich
		Flaps	Set for landing

- At level off, retard throttles to keep speed below V_{lo}.

- Consider early use of intermediate flap to integrate with slower speed circuit traffic if necessary.

- Once the propeller levers and mixture control are fully forward, the approach is controlled in the normal way using pitch to control airspeed and throttles to control height/rate of descent. However, more anticipation of power changes are required due to the greater mass and inertia of the aircraft.

Touch and Go

⇨ Retrim.
⇨ Flaps up.
⇨ Full power.

Go Around

⇨ Pitch to level flight.
⇨ Full power.
⇨ Retract drag flap.
⇨ Pitch for V_y climb.
⇨ Clean up – gear and flaps.
⇨ Re-trim pitch and rudder.

Flapless Landing

⇨ Approach at V_{at} +5kts (*see* Flight Manual).

Short Field Take-Off

Intermediate flap (*see* Flight Manual).
Full power against brake:
⇨ Rotate at V_r −5kts.
⇨ Climb at V_y with full power.
⇨ Return to normal clean profile once obstacle clearance has been achieved.

Short Field Landing

⇨ Approach at V_{at} −5kts (*see* Flight Manual).

AIRMANSHIP	ENGINE HANDLING
Lookout Circuit integration	CHTs Fuel pumps on

MEP Exercise F3: Introduction to Asymmetric Flight

Aim: To control the aircraft in the event of an engine failure, to operate in the asymmetric configuration, and to learn the effect of single-engine operation on performance and systems.

Single-Engine Flight

Configure the aircraft for normal two-engine straight and level flight:
⇨ Shut down and feather an engine (using the appropriate checklist).

Symptoms of Engine Failure

Yaw and roll towards failed engine; pitch down or reduced airspeed.

Instrument indications:

Flight instruments:
- AI – roll to failed engine
- TC – turn to failed engine
- Ball to live engine

Engine instruments:
- MFP + RPM – near normal
- Ts and Ps – near normal
✈ Only fuel flow and EGT give indication

⇨ With the engine shut down, practise the following manoeuvres:

- Straight and level flight
- Climb/descent
- Turns
- Alternate gear and flap lowering
- Flight in the approach configuration
- Alternate gear and flap raising
- Crossfeed operation

Note:
- Reduction of performance
- Yaw trim change with power, speed and configuration change
- Attention to health of live engine
- Time and effort required for manual lowering and raising of gear and flap

⇨ Restart (from checklist).

- Do not retrim:
⇨ Advance throttle (on engine that had been shut down) until yaw trim is restored.
  ✈ This is the 'zero thrust' setting.

Engine Failures in the Cruise

✈ Where recovery to straight and level flight *would not* compromise terrain clearance:

Control – yaw roll and pitch attitude:
⇨ Recover to straight and level flight.

Identify – dead engine.

Verify
⇨ Throttle: idle (dead engine).

Feather
⇨ RPM: feather;
⇨ MIX: cut off.

⇨ Trim – pitch and rudder.
⇨ Checklist drills when stable.

Engine Failure in Different Configurations

- Straight and level

- Climb
  Speed low, power high   ☛ Easy to detect, difficult to control.

- Descent
  Speed high, power low   ☛ Difficult to detect, easy to control.

- Turns
  Failure of inside engine:
      marked roll and yaw   ☛ Easy to detect, difficult to control.
  Failure of outside engine:
      reduced roll and yaw   ☛ Difficult to detect, easy to control.

AIRMANSHIP	ENGINE HANDLING
Lookout Use of trim	Smooth Monitor CHTs

MEP Exercise F4: Critical and Safety Speeds

Aim: To establish V_{mca} and TOSS, and be able to control an engine failure after take-off.

Critical Speeds

V_{mca} Red line speed
↦ *Speed at/above which it should be possible to maintain directional control in the following conditions:*
- Critical engine windmilling
- Max aft C of G
- Max power live engine
- Gear up
- Take-off flap
- Permitted bank

Demonstration in three configurations:

1. Wings level, engine windmilling.
2. Permitted bank, engine windmilling.
3. Permitted bank, zero thrust (may reach V_{so} before V_{mca}; if so, recover at stall).

Entry	During	Recovery

Configure aircraft as above:
⇨ Pitch up
  ☛ Airspeed reduces
	Note:
	  ■ Speed at which directional control is lost
		⇨ Pitch down
		⇨ Close throttles

Take-Off Safety Speed (TOSS)

↦ *Speed at which an average pilot on an average day can suffer an engine failure on take-off and expect to maintain directional control:*
- Conditions as for V_{mca}, except for gear down
↦ i.e. V_{mca}/V_{so} + safe margin for surprise!

Demonstration of two scenarios:

1. Engine failure below TOSS:
  ☛ Recovery below datum altitude.
2. Engine failure above TOSS:
  ☛ Recovery above datum altitude.

Entry	During	Recovery
Configure aircraft as above: ⇨ Initiate normal climb At datum altitude: ⇨ Simulate engine failure	Note: ■ Altitude at which recovery to positive rate of climb is effected	⇨ EFATO drill Climb at best rate of climb speed V_{yse} blue line speed

☙ Engine failure below TOSS is by definition uncontrollable; you therefore have no choice but to close both throttles and land ahead.

EFATO

✈ Where recovery to straight and level flight *would* compromise terrain clearance:

Control – yaw roll and pitch attitude:
    ⇨ Pitch to achieve V_{yse}.

- Power (both engines):
    ⇨ MIX: full rich.
    ⇨ RPM: max.
    ⇨ Throttle: full.

Identify – dead engine.

Verify
    ⇨ Throttle: idle (dead engine).

Feather
    ⇨ RPM: feather (dead engine);
    ⇨ MIX: cut off (dead engine).

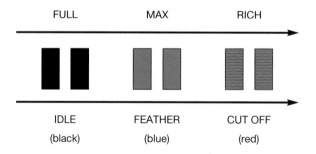

HAND MOVEMENT ACROSS ENGINE CONTROL PEDESTAL

    ⇨ Gear: up
    ⇨ Flaps: up
    ⇨ Cowl flaps: dead, close
                   live, open.

✈ Trim – aileron and rudder.
✈ Checklist drills when stable.

AIRMANSHIP	ENGINE HANDLING
Lookout Awareness of critical speeds	Smooth Monitor CHTs

MEP Exercise F5: Asymmetric Circuits

Aim: To learn to handle an engine failure after take-off, and to carry out an asymmetric circuit, go-around and landing.

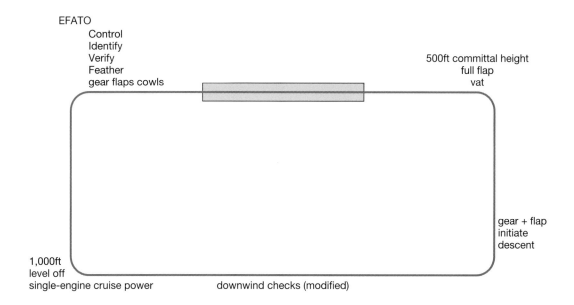

EFATO
Control
Identify
Verify
Feather
gear flaps cowls

500ft committal height
full flap
vat

gear + flap
initiate
descent

1,000ft
level off
single-engine cruise power

downwind checks (modified)

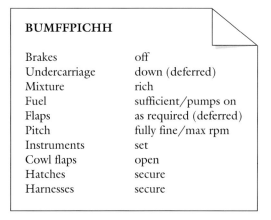

BUMFFPICHH

Brakes	off
Undercarriage	down (deferred)
Mixture	rich
Fuel	sufficient/pumps on
Flaps	as required (deferred)
Pitch	fully fine/max rpm
Instruments	set
Cowl flaps	open
Hatches	secure
Harnesses	secure

➤ High drag items marked 'deferred' should be left until descent is initiated on the base leg.

- Climb straight ahead while completing EFATO drills.

- Consider continuous climbing turn on to downwind leg (to say close to field).

- At level-off reduce MFP, but leave RPM: max; MIX: rich.

- Approach slightly high:
  ✦ Anticipate any undershoot;
  ⇨ Correct early to avoid large power changes.

- Asymmetric committal height – 500ft:
  ⇨ Decide

  ⟳ If approach profile looks OK: ⟳ If approach profile is not OK:
    ⇨ Full flap;   ⇨ Go around.
    ⇨ V_{ap};
    ☛ *You are committed!*
    ⇨ Land.
      [Close both throttles during flare.]

Go Around

  ⇨ Pitch to level flight.
  ⇨ MIX: rich; RPM: max; MFP: full;
    ✦ control yaw.
  ⇨ Gear/flaps up.
  ⇨ Pitch for V_{ysc} climb (<u>blue line speed</u>).
  ⇨ Re-trim pitch and rudder.

Engine Failure below Committal Height

  ⇨ Feather (MFP: idle; RPM: feather; MIX: cut off);
  ⇨ Land.

Aborted Take-Off

  ⇨ Control yaw;
  ⇨ Close both throttles;
  ⇨ Stop.

AIRMANSHIP	ENGINE HANDLING
Control yaw Anticipate power changes	Avoid large power changes

MEP Exercise F6: Asymmetric Performance and Circuits

Aim: To revise the effects of asymmetric operation on performance and systems, and to practise asymmetric circuits.

Performance

Entry	During	Recovery
1. Single-engine straight and level flight: ■ feathered (zero thrust) ■ clean ■ trimmed Note: ■ Power settings ■ Attitude ■ Performance (airspeed) ■ Trim position	⇨ Unfeather (idle thrust) ⇨ Extend gear/flap ✈ (maintain straight and level) Note: ■ Power settings ■ Attitude ■ Performance (airspeed) ■ Trim position	⇨ Recover to normal single-engine straight and level
2. Single-engine climb Note: ■ Rate of climb	⇨ Unfeather ⇨ Extend gear/flap ⇨ Deviation from V_{yse} 　■ V_{yse} +5, +10kts 　■ V_{yse} −5, −10kts Note: ■ Rate of climb	⇨ Recover to normal single-engine climb, then straight and level
3. Single-engine descent Note: ■ Rate of descent	⇨ Repeat as part 2 in descent	⇨ Recover to normal single-engine descent, then straight and level

Systems

Entry	During	Recovery
Two-engine straight and level flight Note: ■ Engine parameters ■ Electrical output/load ■ Fuel flows ⇨ Fail engine ➜ Engine failure drill (actual shutdown using checklist)	Note: ■ Engine parameters ■ Electrical output/load ■ Fuel flows ■ Other system parameters Practise: • Crossfeed • Gear/flap extension/retraction • Other system drills (appropriate to type)	Restart drill from checklist ➜ Allow engine to warm at low power before advancing throttles ⇨ Return to two-engine straight and level flight

Asymmetric Circuit Revision

• EFATO.
• Single-engine approach and landing.
• Go around.

AIRMANSHIP	ENGINE HANDLING
Lookout	Cowl flaps/CHTs Avoid thermal shock to engine during restart

CHAPTER 5

Differences

RETRACTABLE UNDERCARRIAGE

An undercarriage sticking out into the airflow incurs a drag penalty, and it is therefore desirable to retract the undercarriage into the aircraft. However, the retraction mechanism increases the weight, complexity and expense of the aircraft. Since the drag penalty becomes more significant with increasing airspeed, it is usually not worth all the trouble of fitting a retractable undercarriage to a low-speed aircraft. Nevertheless, as design speed increases, the advantages start to outweigh the disadvantages, and a retractable undercarriage becomes viable.

Undercarriage Mechanism

Indications

If the gear is down and locked there are usually three green lights, one for each undercarriage leg.
- Note: The panel lights, when selected on, may dim the undercarriage lights for night flying, and in daylight this may make the lights difficult to see. (This continues to catch people out, making them believe that the gear has not locked down, when in fact it has.)
  ⇨ Turn the panel light off in daylight.

Either gear in transit/unsafe lights, or alternatively gear up and locked lights. There are warning horns if a low power is set with the gear not down.

Controls

There is a gear lever, and most controls will include a down-lock release to stop the gear lever being selected up by accident.
(There may be a downlock release to allow the downlock to be overridden.)

Alternative Gear Lowering

In case the main system fails there may be the following alternatives:
- Manual pump, if the engine pump fails;
- Compressed gas bottle, in case of loss of hydraulic fluid;
- Free fall – releases the uplock (either hydraulic or mechanical) and allows the gear to fall under its own weight; it may be aerodynamically or spring assisted.

Flight Exercise

From straight and level flight:
⇨ reduce speed to V_{le};
⇨ lower gear.
   Note:
   ▪ pitch changes;
   ▪ speed reduction/increase of power required to maintain the desired speed.

   • Climb: note the reduced rate of climb.
   • Descent: note the increased rate of descent.
   • Turns.

⇨ Raise gear (speed below V_{lo}).
   Note:
   • pitch changes;
   • speed increase/reduction of power required to maintain the desired speed.

Alternative Gear Lowering

⇨ Lower (and, if possible, raise) the gear using the back-up gear-lowering mechanism (it may be possible to actually use the back-up systems if the primary system can be bypassed; if not, do as touch drills).
   Note the increased time required to lower the gear.

Approach Configuration

BUMFFPICHH:
⇨ Descend in approach configuration.

The Go-Around

⇨ Pitch to level flight.
⇨ Full power.
⇨ Retract drag flap.
⇨ Pitch for V_y climb.
⇨ Clean up – gear and flaps.
⇨ Re-trim.

Circuits

Practise as necessary.

After Take-Off Checks	
Positive rate of climb:	
Brakes	On/off
Gear	Up
Flaps	Up
Ts and Ps	Green arcs
Power	Climb power
Lights	Off
Above 1,000ft agl:	
Fuel pumps	Off

TAILWHEEL AIRCRAFT

Most aircraft undercarriages consist of three wheels, and associated structures. The two main wheels are designed to support the majority of the aircraft weight, and absorb the forces experienced during landing. In order to do this, they have to be of heavy construction and placed close to the aircraft's centre of gravity. The third wheel supports the aircraft on the ground and takes less of the weight, and so can be of lighter construction. This third wheel can be placed forward of the main wheels to produce a nosewheel aircraft, or aft to produce a tailwheel aircraft.

The nosewheel design has become very much the standard for modern aircraft; however, a nosewheel, as compared with a tailwheel, is a relatively large, and therefore heavy structure, and, as the accident statistics show, relatively vulnerable to mishandling. A tailwheel is comparatively light and rugged, and this makes tailwheel aircraft particularly suitable for strip and rough field operation. Once in the air, a tailwheel aircraft handles no differently to one with a nosewheel, there are however aspects to the design that make the ground handling of a tailwheel aircraft more challenging.

Forward Visibility

Because a tailwheel aircraft sits back on its tailwheel, the nose attitude will be quite high on the ground, creating a blind spot. Depending on the size of the nose and engine this may be quite large, and in order to see forwards while taxiing, the pilot may have to weave the nose from side to side.

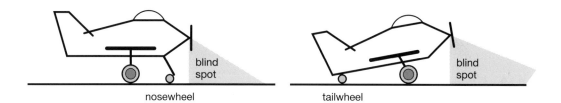

nosewheel   tailwheel

Asymmetric Blade Effect

During take-off in a nosewheel aircraft, the propeller disk will be at approximately 90° to the airflow. During each half revolution each blade will travel the same distance and have the same angle of attack.

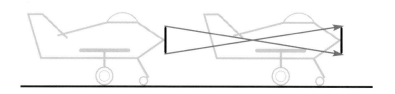

A tailwheel aircraft, on the other hand, has a nose-up pitch attitude on the ground, and the propeller disk is now angled to the airflow. From the diagram it can be seen that the down-going blade now travels a greater distance than the upgoing blade, and has a higher angle of attack, thus producing more thrust. This is called **asymmetric blade effect**.

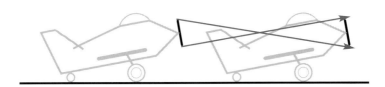

If, as in most aircraft, the propellers rotate clockwise when viewed from behind, the point through which the thrust acts will be displaced to the right, producing a yaw to the left, so the pilot will have to apply right rudder to counteract this. (A right rudder input is required in most nosewheel aircraft to counteract slipstream effects, but the effect is much more marked in a tailwheel aircraft.)

Directional Stability

In order that the aircraft does not tip over when standing on its wheels, the centre of gravity (C of G) must lie somewhere in the triangle formed by the three wheels. As can be seen from the diagrams below, this means that the 'C of G' will be slightly forward of the wheels in a nosewheel aircraft, and slightly aft of the main wheels in a tailwheel aircraft.

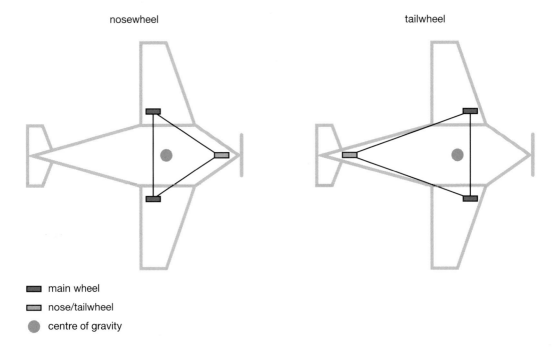

nosewheel   tailwheel

- main wheel
- nose/tailwheel
- centre of gravity

When the aircraft moves along the ground it has inertia, which can be thought of as a force acting in the direction of movement, through the centre of gravity. If the aircraft is then subject to a laterally displacing force (say, a gust of wind) it will tend to pivot about a point approximately midway between the main wheels. From the diagrams below it can be seen that this has the effect of producing a force couple about the pivot point.

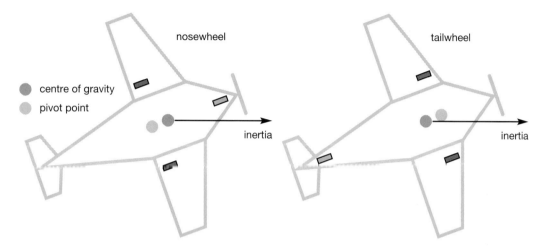

In the case of a nosewheel aircraft, the couple acts to damp the displacement and bring the aircraft back into alignment with the direction of movement. This negative feedback is desirable, and means the aircraft is directionally stable. In the tailwheel case, the force couple acts to accentuate the displacement, which means the aircraft is directionally unstable, and a pilot input will be required to arrest the yaw. If the displacing force is too strong, or the pilot input too little or too late, the aircraft may swing uncontrollably around in a circle: this is called a 'ground loop'.

Taxiing

- Weave the nose to improve forward vision.

- Position control surfaces according to the wind direction, a shown by the diagram. In very light or calm winds, pull the stick back to increase tailwheel steering authority.

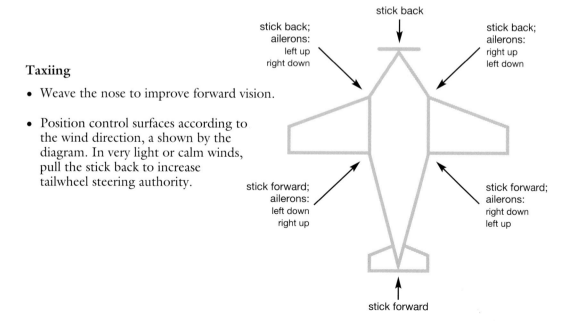

Take-Off

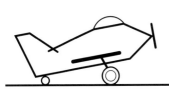 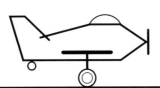 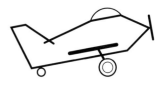

Stick back:
Into wind aileron;
Full power;
⇨ Balance.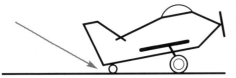

Stick forward:
☛ Tailwheel lifts
   off ground.

At V_r:
Rotate (small
pitch change);
Climb at V_y

Landing

1. Three-point landing	2. Wheeler landing
■ Normal approach. ⇨ At the flare, pitch to the three-point attitude.	■ Normal approach. ⇨ Little flare required to give flat landing attitude.
	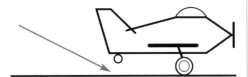
✈ All three wheels should touch the ground simultaneously. ✈ Judge the three-point attitude by noting the nose attitude on the ground before take-off. Once on the ground, stick back.	✈ Main wheels touch down first. ⇨ Stick forward to hold tailwheel off as long as possible. ⇨ Once tailwheel touches down, stick back.

✈ There is no absolute right or wrong answer when considering whether to do a three-point or wheeler landing; a three-point landing increases the effectiveness of tailwheel steering, while a wheeler landing maintains rudder authority longer during the landing roll. Ultimately the choice will be down to the characteristics of the particular aircraft type and, to some degree, personal preference. In the author's personal experience, three point works best on grass, while wheeler works best on tarmac.

VARIABLE PITCH PROPELLERS

Propeller Theory

A propeller blade has an aerofoil section that acts like a rotating wing: instead of providing lift, it provides thrust.
→ Like a wing it is at its most efficient at about a 4° angle of attack.

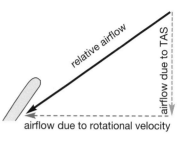

The relative airflow can be determined by the vector summation of the airflow due the rotational velocity of the propeller, and the airflow due to its forward movement through the air (i.e. the aircraft's TAS).

airflow due to rotational velocity

Similar diagrams could be drawn for each phase of operation:

1. Start of take-off run:
   - Full power = high rotational velocity;
   - No forward movement.

relative airflow =
airflow due to rotational velocity

2. Climb:
   - Full power = high rotational velocity;
   - Medium forward TAS.

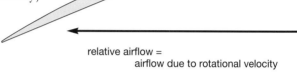

3. Cruise:
   - Medium power = medium rotational velocity;
   - High forward TAS.

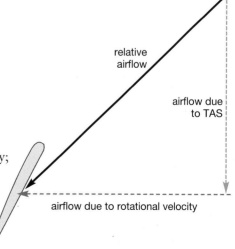
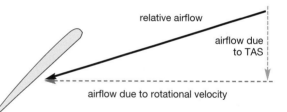

Note that propeller angle in the diagrams above has had to be altered to keep it at the same optimum angle to the relative airflow:
→ fine pitch for take-off and climb;
→ coarse pitch for cruise.
Obviously in simple fixed-pitch aircraft this is not possible; however, the relatively small range of speeds that such aircraft operate within, allows an acceptable compromise angle to be set. As aircraft become faster, such a compromise becomes less acceptable, and the extra weight and expense of a variable pitch propeller is justified.
■ The variable pitch propeller extends propeller efficiency over a greater range of speeds.

Constant Speed Units

The propeller pitch is governed by a constant speed unit, which the pilot controls by setting a desired RPM using the propeller lever. A detailed description of a constant speed unit is outside the scope of this book; however, the constant speed unit automatically adjusts pitch with variations of power and airspeed to maintain a given RPM, thus allowing the propeller to operate more efficiently at any combination of selected RPM, power and airspeed.

Feathering

When the throttle is retarded to the idle position, or if engine failure occurs, the propeller may continue to turn, or 'windmill', because of the airflow over it. The diagram shows that the low rotational velocity, and still relatively high airspeed, combine to produce a negative angle of attack. In this situation, negative thrust or drag is produced. During an approach this may be useful; however, in the event of an engine failure it is most unwelcome.

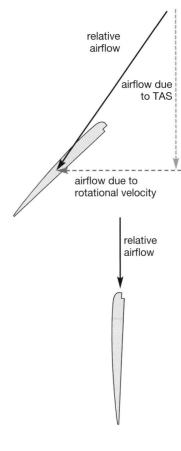

relative airflow

airflow due to TAS

airflow due to rotational velocity

relative airflow

To prevent this, constant speed units are fitted with a feather mechanism that drives the propeller beyond the normal coarse setting until edge on to the airflow. This stops the propeller turning and leaves it in the minimum drag position. The feathering mechanism is an electrically driven, high-pressure oil pump, or accumulator, and is activated by retarding the propeller lever through the 'feathering gate' (some aircraft, mainly older designs, may have a separate feathering switch or button).

Some constant speed units are fitted with pitch latches, which operate if the RPM falls below a certain limit, to prevent the propeller feathering. This is advantageous in the case of a normal ground shut-down, as starting an engine with a feathered propeller puts considerable strain on the starter and battery. The problem arises if, following an engine failure, the propeller is not feathered promptly and RPM decays below the speed at which the latches engage, thus preventing the propeller feathering.
→ Should this occur, opening the throttle on the failed engine will recover 100 to 300rpm and allow feathering to proceed.

Handling: Controls and Indications

For a simple fixed-pitch aircraft, power relates directly to engine RPM, and therefore a throttle and RPM gauge are all that is necessary. Obviously with a variable pitch propeller fit, the constant speed unit maintains the RPM selected by the pilot, irrespective of power setting, and so an alternative indication of power is required. For piston aircraft this is usually in the form of a manifold pressure gauge. In addition, leaning the engine cannot be done with reference to RPM, so a fuel flow gauge is also provided.

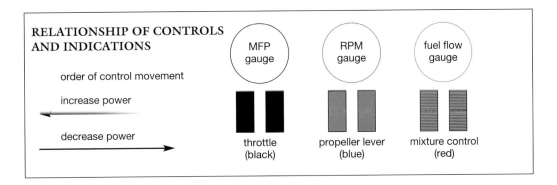

A situation can be envisaged where the throttle is advanced, without advancing the propeller lever, to such an extent that the constant speed unit is unable to absorb the power output. Thus in order to avoid excessive stress on the constant speed unit:
→ RPM should be increased before increasing power; and
→ power should be reduced before reducing RPM.

The exact setting of mixture, RPM and MFP, for various phases of flight, will be detailed in the flight manual. In some aircraft the mixture setting may be done by reference to an exhaust gas temperature gauge, rather than using fuel flows.

Flight Exercises

Power Checks

The check will include the following, in addition to the usual items:

Throttle   Appropriate setting

➜ *rpm within constant speed range.*
Propeller lever   Exercise ×3, max
                            drop 300rpm
➜ *to circulate oil through the CSU.*

Throttle   Appropriate setting
➜ *rpm below constant speed range.*
Propeller lever   Check feathering
                            action
➜ *Retard prop lever to feathering gate –*
  no rpm reduction;
➜ *retard through gate – engine should*
  start to feather;
➜ *quickly return prop lever through gate*
  before feathering completes so as not
  to stress engine.

Taxiing
MIX: rich, RPM: max
Control speed with throttle as normal.

Take-Off
MIX: rich, RPM: top of green arc:
Throttle: T/o power setting:
⇨ Set climb power (MFP RPM MIX).

Climb
Power (MIX RPM MFP);
Attitude;
Trim.

➜ MFP reduces by approx 1in per 1,000ft:
  ⇨ Reset MFP.

Level Off
Attitude – allow aircraft to accelerate;
Power (MFP RPM MIX);
Trim.

Descending
Power (MFP RPM MIX);
Attitude;
Trim.

➜ MFP increases by approx 1in per
  1,000ft:
  ⇨ Reset MFP.

Level off
Power (MIX RPM MFP);
Attitude – allow aircraft to accelerate;
Trim.

Approach
BUMFFPICHH
⇨ MIX: rich, RPM: max.
Approach is then controlled normally
with the throttle.

Go Around
Throttle: T/o power setting:
(MIX: rich RPM: max, already set).
Once aircraft is clean and climbing:
⇨ Set climb power (MFP RPM MIX).

Stalling
MIX: rich, RPM: max
Control with throttle as normal.

Engine failure
To feather engine (touch drill).

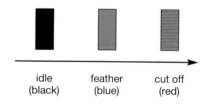

idle   feather   cut off
(black)   (blue)   (red)

SUPER AND TURBO CHARGING

The power output of a piston engine is proportional to the mass of the charge (the fuel air mixture) burnt in the cylinder. For a given size of cylinder the maximum charge is dependent on the air pressure in the induction manifold, which, for a normally aspirated engine, is a function of ambient atmospheric pressure.

If, however, the manifold pressure (MFP) is artificially 'boosted' by pressurizing the air in the induction manifold, the engine's power output will be increased. To do this, a compressor (usually a centrifugal compressor) is placed in the induction airflow upstream of the induction manifold. If the compressor is driven by an auxiliary drive from the engine, it is called a supercharger; if driven by a turbine in the exhaust gas flow, it's called a turbocharger. Various configurations are possible, such as multiple stage compressors, and the use of intercoolers (between the compressors) and aftercoolers (downstream of the last compressor) to cool the air and make it even more dense.

The pilot directly controls the MFP with the throttle; however, the amount of boost is also affected by compressor RPM. Since in a supercharger this is directly related to engine RPM, it is necessary to set RPM first with the prop lever, then set power with the throttle. For a turbocharger (*see* diagram) the compressor speed is controlled by the waste gate valve, which determines the amount of exhaust gas that is routed either to the turbine, or through the bypass duct. The position of the waste gate is governed by a pressure sensor, the density controller, in the compressor discharge airflow, so the system acts to maintain the MFP set by the pilot.

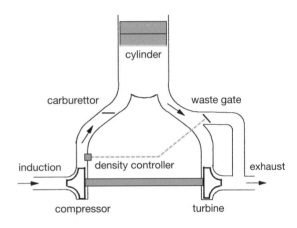

On the ground, the supercharger or turbocharger is capable of supplying more air than required, which, if the throttle were fully opened, would result in overboosting and possible engine damage. As a result, the throttle will usually be less than fully open on take-off. As the aircraft climbs, ambient pressure will slowly decrease (approx. 1in per 1,000ft), resulting in a drop of MFP, so the throttle valve will need to be opened to compensate. Depending on the aircraft fit, this may be taken care of automatically, or be done manually by the pilot. Eventually an altitude is reached when the throttle valve is fully opened, the 'full throttle altitude'; further climb will result in a reduction of MFP.

Controls and Indications

The general layout of the controls and their related gauges will be similar to a variable pitch prop aircraft (*see* page 113):
- mixture control and fuel flow gauge;
- prop lever and RPM gauge;
- throttle and manifold pressure gauge.
  The manifold pressure gauge may be calibrated for absolute pressure, or boost pressure, i.e. to read zero at mean sea-level pressure.
- Overboost warning lights, or there may be a way of presetting a maximum MFP.
- Manual waste-gate control on some older turbochargers.

Handling

Again, handling is generally similar to a VP prop aircraft, in that settings for mixture, RPM and MFP, for different phases of flight, will be as stated in the flight manual. The main difference will be when setting take-off power, now done relative to the MFP gauge, rather than by simply pushing the throttle fully forwards. Particular care will also be needed setting power for a go-around, when it is very easy to inadvertently overboost in all the excitement.

APPENDIX I
Checklists

An aircraft checklist comprises a list of logically sequenced actions required to ensure the safe operation of the aircraft. The overall checklist is broken down into a series of sub-lists, each to be performed at different phases of flight. For single pilot, single engine operation, there are two generally accepted methods to action a list:

1. By direct reference to the checklist; used when the aircraft is on the ground and stationary. These checks tend to be relatively long.
2. From memory; to allow lookout and instrument scan to be maintained. Mnemonics are often used to help the pilot remember memory checklists.

In civilian/sport aviation, checklists tend to be used as 'do' lists: you refer to the checklist and then perform the action. This is entirely reasonable, given that a good percentage of recreational pilots are infrequent flyers and could not be expected to be able to perform the whole operation from memory. The alternative philosophy (favoured, among others, by the military) is to do all the required actions first, then refer to the checklist to check you haven't missed anything.

On the following pages is a generic checklist for the normal operation of a 'simple' (fixed pitch prop, fixed undercarriage) light aircraft to illustrate the order of checks, and to group together the memory checks to aid learning. Other normal operation checks are included at the end.

BEFORE START

Seats	Adjusted and locked
Hatches and harnesses	Secure
Park brake	On
Master switch	On
Circuit breakers	All in
Instruments	Serviceable and legible
Radios	Off
Fuel	On, check contents, select appropriate tank
Flying controls	Full and free, correct sense
Trims	Full and free, set for t/o (electric trim)
Flaps	Check, then up
Heaters and vents	Closed

STARTING

Beacon	On
Mixture controls	Full and free, max rich
Throttle friction	Loose
Throttle	Full and free, set 1in open
Carb heat	Full and free, set cold
(Fuel pump	On, check press, off)
Primer	Prime as required, lock
Lookout	Call 'Clear Prop'
Magnetos	On, operate starter

AFTER START

Starter light	Out
RPM	1,200
Oil pressure	Rising within 30 sec.
Ammeter	Charging
Suction	Check
Magnetos	Check dead cut
Flight instruments	Set, gyros synchronized
Radio/navaids	On, turned and checked
Altimeters	Set QFE/QNH
Taxi clearance	

Taxi Checks

Brake	(in clear area)
Turn:	nosewheel steering
Left	Compass/DI – decreasing
Right	Compass/DI – increasing
AI	level
TC	turn indicated

POWER CHECKS

Position	Into wind, clear all round
Brakes	On
(Fuel	Select fuller tank)
Ts and Ps	Check
Throttle	Appropriate setting
Carb heat	Hot, check rpm drop, cold
Magnetos	Dead cut, check rpm, drop
Suction	Check
Ammeter	Charging
Ts and Ps	Check within limits
Throttle	Idle, check slow running, reset 1,200rpm

PRE-TAKE-OFF

Trim	Set for t/o
Throttle friction	Set
Mixture	Rich
Magnetos	On
Primer	Locked
Pitot heat	On
Fuel	On (fullest tank)
(Fuel pumps	On)
Flaps	Set for t/o
Instruments/ radios	Checked and set
Hatches and harnesses	Closed and secure
Carb heat	Cold
Flying Controls	Full and free

After Take-Off Checks

Flaps	Up
Ts and Ps	Green arcs
Power	Climb power
Lights	Off

Above 1,000ft agl

Fuel pumps	Off (unless staying in the circuit)

CRUISE CHECKS

FREDA

Fuel	Tank/pump/sufficient
Radio	Freq/standby
Engine	Ts and Ps/carb heat
Direction indicator	Synchronized
Altimeter	Pressure setting

DOWNWIND CHECKS

BUMFFPICHH

Brakes	Off
Undercarriage	Down
Mixture	Rich
Fuel	Sufficient/pumps on
Flaps	As required
Pitch	Fixed/max rpm
Instruments	Set QFE
Carb heat	Checked hot
Hatches	Secure
Harnesses	Secure

AFTER LANDING CHECKS

Carb heat	Cold
Flaps	Up
Fuel pumps	Off
Unnecessary electrics, radio/ nav aids	All off

SHUTDOWN

Position	Into wind
Park brake	On
Throttles	1,200rpm for 30sec
Radios/navaids	Off
Magnetos	Dead cut
Throttles	Closed
Mixture	Idle cut off
Magnetos	Off
Beacon/electrics	Off
Master switch	Off

PRE-STALLING OR AEROBATICS

HASELL

Height	Sufficient to recover by 2,500ft
Airframe	As required
Security	Hatches/harnesses/ loose articles
Engine	Ts and Ps/carb heat
Location	Clear of cloud/ controlled airspace/ built-up areas
Lookout	Especially below – clearing turns.

CHECKS FOR MORE COMPLEX AIRCRAFT

Power checks for an aeroplane with variable pitch propellers:

Position	Into wind, clear all round
Brakes	On
(Fuel	Select fuller tank)
Ts and Ps	Check
Throttle	Appropriate setting
Prop lever	Exercise ×3, check max drop
Magnetos	Dead cut, check rpm drop
Alternate Air	Open, close, negligible drop
Suction	Check
Alternator	Check output
Ts and Ps	Check within limits
Throttle	Appropriate setting
Prop lever	Check feathering action
Throttle	Idle, check slow running, reset 1,200rpm

Pre-landing checks for an aeroplane with variable pitch propellers and retractable undercarriage:

Pre-Landing Checks

Reds	MIX: rich
Blues	RPM: Max
Greens	Gear down and locked
Or	
PUFF	
Pitch	RPM: Max
Undercarriage	Gear down and locked
Fuel	MIX: rich
Flaps	Set for landing

CHECKS ASSOCIATED WITH IMC

Cruise checks in IMC:

FREDAI

Fuel	Tank/pump/sufficient
Radio	Freq/standby
Engine	Ts and Ps/carb heat
Direction indicator	Synchronized
Altimeter	Pressure setting
Ice	

Turning over a Beacon (procedural approach)

TTTT

Time	Start watch
Twist	Heading bug
Turn	Initiate
Talk	ATC

Emergencies

Emergencies fall into two categories: those you need to do something about right now, for example, fire or engine failure; and those you don't, for example, electrical or radio failure. For the less urgent emergencies, it may be best to stabilize the aircraft, then refer to the checklist; however, for emergencies requiring immediate response, the appropriate actions will have to carried out from memory. For 'simple' single-engine piston aircraft, checklists tend to be either memory checklists, or ones that should be referred to. As aircraft get more complicated the checklist may become hybrid – it may contain a number of memory items that are then followed by a direct reference section.

Notwithstanding the advice given in any checklist, the general principle for dealing with any unexpected situation is to 'aviate', 'navigate' and 'communicate':

- **Aviate**: Fly the aircraft and maintain flying airspeed; it's better to hit the ground in a controlled way while still flying, than stall in from altitude.
- **Navigate**: Steer away from danger and towards an airfield if possible.
- **Communicate**: ATC may be able to help, but in the worst case scenario, organize the rescue services to get to where you expect to come down.

AVIATE.   NAVIGATE.   COMMUNICATE.

MEMORY CHECKLIST FOR EMERGENCIES IN A SINGLE-ENGINE PISTON AIRCRAFT

Fire on the Ground

Throttle	Close
⇨ Stop aircraft	
Mixture	Idle cut off
☛ Engine stops	
Fuel/pumps	Off
Mags	Off
(Mayday if time available)	
Master	Off
⇨ Evacuate upwind, taking fire extinguisher with you	

Engine Fire in Flight

Fuel/pumps	Off
Cabin heaters/air	Closed
☛ Engine stops	
Throttle	Close
Mags	Off
Mixture	Idle cut off
⇨ Forced landing	

Electrical Fire in Flight

Master	Off
Switches	Off
Heaters and vents	Close
Fire extinguisher	Use as necessary
⇨ Ventilate cabin	

Ditching

Mayday	
Harness	Tight
Door/windows	Unlatched/open
Large swell/light wind	Land along swell
Strong wind/small swell	Land into wind
Use life jackets/rafts once outside cabin	

Engine Failure after Take-Off (EFATO)

Attitude	Best glide airspeed
Trim	
Select field within 30° of nose	
☠ Do not turn back	
Mayday	
Fuel	Off
Mixture	Idle cut off
Mags	Off
Master	Off
(if electric flaps, leave on until final flap selection)	
Door	Unlatched
Harness	Tight
Flaps	As required

Engine Failure at Altitude

Attitude	Best glide airspeed
Trim	
Select field	
Plan approach/1,000ft point	
Fault find	
Fuel	On/sufficient
Mixture	Rich
Ts and Ps	Check
Mags	On both
Master	On
Primer	Locked
Attempt restart	
Mayday	
Shut down	
Fuel	Off
Mixture	Idle cut off
Mags	Off
Master	Off
(if electric flaps, leave on until final flap selection)	
Door	Unlatched
Harness	Tight
Flaps	As required

APPENDIX III
Phonetic Alphabet and Morse Code

Letter	Word	Morse
A	Alpha	• —
B	Bravo	— • • •
C	Charlie	— • — •
D	Delta	— • •
E	Echo	•
F	Foxtrot	• • — •
G	Golf	— — •
H	Hotel	• • • •
I	India	• •
J	Juliet	• — — —
K	Kilo	— • —
L	Lima	• — • •
M	Mike	— —
N	November	— •
O	Oscar	— — —
P	Papa	• — — •
Q	Quebec	— — • —
R	Romeo	• — •
S	Sierra	• • •
T	Tango	—
U	Uniform	• • —
V	Victor	• • • —
W	Whiskey	• — —
X	X-ray	— • • —
Y	Yankee	— • — —
Z	Zulu	— — • •

Q codes

QFE	Pressure setting which datums altimeter to airfield height.
QNH	Pressure setting which datums altimeter to mean sea level.
QDM	Magnetic bearing to the station.
QDR	Magnetic bearing from the station.
QUJ	True bearing to the station.
QTE	True bearing from the station.
QGH	Approach based on headings to steer supplied by ATC.

APPENDIX IV
V Speeds

V_2	Take-off safety speed
V_a	Max rough air speed
V_{ap}	Approach speed
V_{at}	Threshold speed
V_{fe}	Max flap extension speed
V_{le}	Max gear extension speed
V_{lo}	Max gear retraction speed
V_{mca}	Min control speed – air
V_{ne}	Never exceed speed
V_{no}	Max normal operation speed
V_r	Rotation speed
V_{si}	Stall speed – flap up (in)
V_{so}	Stall speed – flap down (out)
V_x	Best angle of climb speed
V_{xse}	Best angle of climb speed – single engine
V_y	Best rate of climb speed
V_{yse}	Best rate of climb speed – single engine

Squawk Codes

7000	Conspicuity
7500	Hijack
7600	Radio failure
7700	Emergency

Glossary

A/c	aircraft		GA	General Aviation
a/s	airspeed		G-registered	aircraft registered in the UK
ADF	automatic direction finding		GS	groundspeed
agl	above ground level			
AI	attitude indicator		Hdg	heading
Alt	altimeter/altitude		HSI	horizontal situation indicator
AME	authorized medical examiner			
ANO	air navigation order		ICO	idle cut off
APT	Attitude, Power, Trim		IFR	instrument flight rules
ASI	air speed indicator		ILS	instrument landing system
ATC	Air Traffic Control		IMC	instrument meteorological conditions
ATPL	airline transport pilot's licence		inc	increase
			IR	instrument rating
BBB	Bank, Balance, Back pressure			
			JAA	Joint Aviation Authority
C of G	centre of gravity		JAR	Joint Aviation Requirements
CAA	Civil Aviation Authority		JAR-FCL	JAR-Flight Crew Licensing
Carb	carburettor			
Cb	cumulonimbus (cloud)		kts	knots (nautical miles per hour)
Cb Ht	carburettor heat			
CDI	course deviation indicator			
CHT	cylinder-head temperature		Ldg	landing
CPL	commercial pilot's licence			
			m	metres (measurement)
dec	decrease		MA	missed approach
DI	direction indicator		Mags	magnetos
DME	distance measuring equipment		MAP	missed approach point
			MAUW	maximum all-up weight
DR	dead reckoning		MEP	multi-engine piston
DVLA	Driver and Vehicle Licensing Authority		MFP	manifold pressure
			min	minimum
EFATO	engine failure after take-off		MIX	mixture
EGT	exhaust gas temperature		ML	medium level (turn)
			MLW	max landing weight
FRTO	flight radio telephony operator		MSA	minimum safe altitude
ft	feet (measurement)		MTOW	max take-off weight
FTO	flight training organization			

NDB	non-directional beacon		**sec**	second (time)
NPPL	national private pilot's licence		**SEP**	single-engine piston
			sim	simulator
nm	nautical miles		**SRA**	surveillance radar approach
			SVFR	special Visual Flight Rules
OBI	omni-bearing indicator			
OBS	omni-bearing selector		**TAS**	true airspeed
OCH	obstacle clearance height		**T/o**	take-off
			T/S	turn and slip (*see* TC)
PAPI	precision approach path indicators		**TC**	turn co-ordinator (*see* T/S)
			TOSS	take-off safety speed
PAR	precision approach radar		**Ts & Ps**	temperatures and pressures
PAT	Power, Attitude, Trim			
Pax	passengers		**VASIS**	visual approach slope indicating system
PEC	pressure error correction			
PIC	pilot in command		**VDF**	VHF direction finding
POB	people on board		**VFR**	visual flight rules
PPL	private pilot's licence		**VHF**	very high frequency
PPR	prior permission required		**VMC**	visual meteorological conditions
Pwr	power			
			VOR	VHF omnidirectional range (beacon)
RBI	relative bearing indicator			
RMI	radio magnetic indicator		**VP**	variable pitch (propeller)
RoC	rate of climb		**VSI**	vertical speed indicator
RoD	rate of descent			
RPM	revs per minute		**w/s**	wind speed
RT	radio telephony			
			x-wind	crosswind
S&L	straight and level			